W0017418

365 Ways To Take Control of Your Mental Health

One Revolutionary Concept a Day to
Create the Life You Desire

TAYLOR FISCHER

ISBN 978-1-66781-775-0 eBook 978-1-66781-776-7

Contents

I DEDICATE THIS BOOK to all those who have ever felt suicidal or homicidal. You are not alone. There is so much more to the world and yourself than what you are feeling right now, and you have the power to have it.

Authors Note

This book is a collection of things I learned on my way to finding peace. I do not have any formal education on the subject. However, I believe we all have something to learn from each other. I hope some of the lessons I learned, and share will provide you value. I hope that by reading this book you do not have to go through pain that I endured. I hope that you never lose control and that if you are on that path this book serves as a guide to bring you back.

This book is organized into 3 major sections. These sections have many subjects in them, and the subjects are broken into much smaller parts. They often explain the why, what, or how individually. I've done this because I believe that learning to break down our thought process' and behaviors into these smaller pieces gives us the power to understand, control, and change our actions.

I've written this is 2nd person because I am talking to people. You are a person; I am a person. We are all real and valid. I don't want this to seem like a disconnected manual to life because the purpose of this book is to find deeper connection.

Some of the things stated in this book may seem like common sense, but not all "common" ideas are common to all. So, this book serves a starting point to creating a culture for people who have not been exposed to ideas that propel them forward or expand their outlook on life.

For the best experience with this book I recommend first reading through it fully, so you will have the complete picture on what each point entails, and all the following information that may apply to that point. Then you may go through one point at a time per day and reflect on it and in what ways taking action on it may add value to improve your life.

Please read the closing remarks, about the author, and #365mental health for the complete picture of this book.

A. Finding your peace

When utilized correctly the mind is the most powerful tool we are gifted with. But when we are unable to control it the thoughts we it becomes our biggest burden. This section addresses that. I believe the foundation to reaching your highest level of satisfaction begins with creating internal peace.

Mental Health as a Journey

1. **The Journey of your mind**-Being in a state where you're emotionally and mentally at peace does not happen overnight. It's a journey, and like any journey it has highs and lows. It involves creating productive habits and removing destructive habits. It will be challenging, and you must prepare yourself for it, but it is a necessity. You deserve peace. You must find what works for you and do it. In this chapter are some thoughts to consider along that journey.

2. **Your duty to yourself**-There are countless reasons that you may decide to focus your attention on mental health, or personal and spiritual growth. But just like any other goal you first and foremost must be doing it for yourself. This is not something you can't neglect. You owe it to yourself to begin this journey. You owe it to the past version of yourself that has endured so much, you owe it to the present version of yourself that deserves to enjoy the best of every moment, and you owe it to the future version of yourself that deserves a future of limitless possibilities.

3. **Deciding to take control of your mental health**-If you want to achieve results in anything you must make it a priority. Mental Health is no different. Taking control of your mental health is something that you must commit to. During the easy times, during

the hard times, and during the uncertain times you have to stay committed to yourself and the idea of improving your mentality.

4. **Don't be afraid to ask for help**-Few things are an individual effort. Even though your journey is about you, it still does not mean you have to find all the solutions on your own. If you feel overwhelmed, lost, or unmotivated you should find a person, group, or outlet to lean on. Something to hold you accountable to your commitment and inspire you to remember why you started this journey.

5. **Personal development vessels**- When people think about personal growth and mental help, they think in a box that society has set for them in regard to how they are supposed to go about it. Personal growth is about finding your grounding, challenging yourself, and expanding your mind. This has an endless number of forms. What it is to one person may not be the same as what it is to another. The examples vary, it could be reading, or watching motivating content. It may be spending time in company that inspires you or talking to a licensed therapist. It might even be something that keeps you active with a busy mind like working on a project, running, or yoga. Likely it is a combination of some of the stated ideas along with your own spin on what works best for you. Don't limit any aspect of your growth to a bubble.

6. **A challenging journey**-As stated before, growing your mind and soul is challenging. Any time you take yourself out of a place of comfort and predictability you will experience resistance. You may experience it from yourself, or you may experience it from those who are witnessing you change. To become who you desire to be you must be resilient. You will have to weather many storms. This is a forewarning to open your mind to the struggles you may face as you break from your mold and recreate yourself into who you deserve to be. A person who is complete.

Mental Health as a practice

7. **Your practice**-Your journey is a practice. Like any practice you are not going to achieve perfection overnight. You likely won't get the first attempt right. You will move forward, and then backwards at times, but if you commit yourself to this practice then your over-all trajectory will be one that is forward moving. The practice of mental health begins with having a flexible mind. With time and persistence, the things that you learn will empower you to solve future problems.

8. **The practitioners mind**-Your relationship to your growth will fluctuate. You will experience a broad range of different emotions during the journey both good and bad. This is part of the storm that you must weather. Initially your feelings may be intense and unpredictable, but as you grow more experienced and develop a deeper connection with yourself you should begin to gain more and more control over your thoughts. As this happens you will pro-portionately obtain control over yourself, and in turn your future.

9. **Climbing the mountain**-What matters most is that your overall direction is a positive one. It may not feel like it all the time, but you will begin to notice that even though you still experience low points, they are not as hopeless as previous lows you have experi-enced. Through consistent practice you will find less variance in your direction, and more power to mold your outcome.

10. **Building your toolbox**-Throughout the practice of this journey you will gain skills and understanding that will empower you to manifest your desires into reality. This is a never-ending process. That is one of the purposes of this book. To give you a starting point for that practice by supplying you with a toolbox. So, whether it's from this book or another source when you consume information

add it to your toolbox and rest assured that the compound experience throughout time will give you so many solutions and skills. Eventually, you will solve problems before they occur.

The language of mental health

11. **The Power of Language**-The language you use is an indicator of your feelings. Become aware of the language you are using and the language that you should use to create the outcome you want. The language you use about yourself, your problems, and the world is either going to distract and limit you or guide and empower you.

12. **Understand the language**-Every subject has its own language. The more time you spend around an environment the more you hear certain words. These words will not only help you understand what you are talking about, but they will also guide you to think a certain way. This is why it's so important to begin to consider the language you use and what it is doing for you.

13. **Language and perception**-The language you use about yourself, the world, and your life both reflects and creates your outlook on these subjects. Disparaging statements point out problems without allowing you to be creative or make solutions. Positive language on the other hand will foster a productive environment for you by giving you understanding and optimism.

14. **Distracting language**-When you make a mistake and refer to yourself in a derogatory way. This is a dead-end statement. This language will distract you from empowering yourself to grow. For example, stating "I'm lazy." Or "I didn't wake up on time because I'm lazy." Is distracting language. It shuts down your brain before you are implored to deeper consider your actions and the feelings that motivate them.

15. **Enabling language**-Language that enable you is often open ended or provides a solution that guides you to proper action. They motivate you to think and ask questions. If you were to state: "Why do I keep failing to wake up?" or "I don't wake up because I am not passionate about my day." You would have answers and solutions that direct you in ways that you can act upon.

16. **The language of maturity**-At first you will not be conscious of how your language affects you, and when you become conscious of it you will frequently find yourself violating the boundaries you set for yourself. But as you grow it will be a conscious effort to use language that supports you. As your evolution progresses you will find that you no longer consider using distracting language. When enabling language becomes second nature you will find all other aspects of your life correspondingly improve, because the language you use is an example of the love, excitement, and understanding you have for yourself, as well as the rest of the world

Your relationship to yourself

17. **What is your relationship with yourself**-As humans it is natural to consider your relationship with those around you. How you behave and interact with others. But how often do you consider your relationship with yourself? This is the first and most important relationship you must consider. Like any other relationship you need to give the relationship you have with yourself time, attention, and consideration. The reward is a higher quality of life. Becoming more connected with yourself will reduce a lot of the distractors that you face internally on a day to day basis. It will also improve your clarity and happiness as you stop fighting yourself and start working with yourself.

18. **How do you view yourself-**One of the most vital questions you need to explore when considering your relationship to yourself is how do you view yourself? Are you proud of the person you look at in the mirror? Are you understanding towards that person? Do you love and support that person? Consider being on the opposite end of the spectrum. Being constantly disappointed in yourself, not understanding your feelings or actions, hating, and not believing in yourself. That would be a terrible way to live. But many people are living that way. You may be one of them. That is what this book is for. To help you change your perception of yourself and the world around you. Begin by paying attention now to how you behave towards yourself.

19. **Take the awkwardness out of life-**In order to change your perspective on something you must first understand it. This is the same in regard to yourself. Dig deeper and ask yourself "WHY?" As you ask yourself why you behave and think in certain ways you will uncover the core of who you are and how you became to be that way. Understanding your motivations is important. Once you understand them others may understand them too. If you cannot understand your motivations, then this may be a clue that you may be doing things for the wrong reason. By understanding yourself you can forgive, love, and improve yourself.

20. **The double-edged sword-**How you view others is often a direct reflection of how you view yourself. If you hold on to the short comings of others, then you will likely hold on to your own short-comings. No one deserves this burden. When you open yourself to accepting the imperfections of others you allow yourself to accept your own imperfections and vice versa.

21. **Love yourself-**Accept yourself for who you've been, who you are and who you will be. Each one leads to the next. Do not degrade

yourself by using comparisons of present self with who you were or who you want to be. What matters is who you are now and how you intend to be the next version of yourself. Your past is a detail that guided you to where you are now. Every single one of these versions of who you are deserves love. You cannot love one side of yourself unless you love them all, because this is loving the whole and complete picture of who you are.

22. **The Practice of Self Love**-Loving yourself is more than an idea, it is a set of actions. Think about your ideal relationship and how you would like to be treated. Do for yourself what you would want others to do for you, or what you would do for someone you loved unconditionally. Make it a habit to do things you enjoy, treat yourself special occasionally, and listen to your needs.

Distractors

23. **A path of distractions**-On the path to finding inner peace and self-control you will face many distractions. This section is made to help identify some of the obstacles you may come across, so that if you face them, you are more equipped to overcome them. You will see there is a wide range of distractions you can encounter. If you find yourself at a crossroads that you cannot seem to pass, consider what kind of distraction you may be running into. The most important part of overcoming a distraction is identifying what it is and taking the time to address it.

24. **The fear of missing out**-Fear and greed facilitate some of the most illogical and least thought-out decisions. When you find yourself under pressure to make a decision, stop. Reflect and understand where your motivations coming from. When you are afraid of missing out or struggling, you lower yourself to the point of desperation. Desperation takes your power and judgement away from

you and causes irrational behavior. When you are faced with this crossroad take time to reflect on the abundancy of opportunity that exists in the world.

25. **Overcoming your inner child**-People learn much of their behaviors as children. They learn habits, communication, coping mechanisms, and more. Many people will use the things they learned before adolescence for the rest of their lives. They never advance their behavior to thinking further than what they learned as a child. If you do this, it will keep you from communicating with yourself and others as clearly and affectively as you could be. Pay attention to your behaviors and make sure they properly reflect your life experiences, your growth, and your intentions.

26. **Negative reinforcement**-People's behaviors are encouraged or dejected by the reaction they receive for their actions. When someone receives negative reinforcement, they may hold the event close to the heart. They might carry what should have been a learning experience as a sign that they are not meant to do something. Only you decide what you are meant to do. Do not let your path be limited by negative reinforcement.

27. **Getting the right things in the wrong way**-People crave positive reinforcement. But remember the people that you may receive positive reinforcement from are also flawed. Just because your behavior is encouraged does not mean it is the right or best way to do things. Reflect and hold yourself accountable separate from what others encourage you to do.

28. **Evading the negativity of others**-Its natural to search for guidance from other people. Ironically people accept advice from others who don't even have similar aspirations. This isn't always a bad thing. But caution yourself. Some people who have failed to grow will

discourage you from growing. They will only have negative things to tell you. Be careful of this trap. If you surround yourself with the consultation of too many people like this, you may also find yourself stagnating or regressing.

29. **Information overload**-Educating yourself before you start something is a good idea. However, a distraction that many people run into is getting overwhelmed by too much information. This can become confusing. You will never learn everything, and nothing teaches like real experience. If you wait until you know everything to start your project you will find yourself putting off your start day, day after day, and week after week. It can even become an unconscious crutch.

30. **Perfection paralysis**-Its normal to want to get things right when doing anything. That being said if you notice yourself being afraid to do something because you don't want to fail or get something wrong, you need to take a step back. The only certainty is that you will get something wrong. This is the best way to grow. No one who has become successful has done such without getting something wrong. So, dive in.

Guilt

31. **Everyone is guilty**-Everyone feels shame over something. One may rebuttal that their error was much greater than someone else's or that no one has made their mistake before. It does not negate the fact that everyone has fallen short, and that every person is imperfect. This is a natural part of the human experience. No one mistake outweighs another because the essence of mistakes at the core all come from the same place which is an imperfect human nature. It does not matter that the effects of one fault are greater or longer lasting than another. It all comes from the same design.

32. **The key is growth**-The only thing that one should be expected to do is to acknowledge and learn from their transgressions. By acknowledging your faults, you do yourself and others the service of placing your ego and emotions aside to accept your misconduct and the effects that they may have caused. From that point you can administer the practice of education to ensure that you grow away from the behavior that caused your wrongdoing. This process may take longer in some than others.

33. **Self-sabotage**-We all have our own self-perception. One of the worst forms of self-sabotage is to allow your self-image to come from a shortcoming that you have had. When you identify your whole life based off a short coming you sell yourself short. Often people assume that everyone sees them only as the blemished person that they see themselves as. This is untrue, people will view you based on how you make them feel and how you behave in your day to day interactions, above all else. Often people see you for your strengths while you are still limited to seeing yourself as a reflection of your flaws.

34. **You are limitless**-You chose what you are known for both to yourself and others. You can reframe the image that you have of yourself to one that empowers you rather than hinders you. Your shortcomings are the building blocks to becoming the most quintessential version you can be.

35. **Be forward thinking**-Instead of being concerned about who you were and what you did, focus on what you want to be, and what you need to do to get there. Plan backwards from who and where you want to be.

Judgement

36. **Origins of judgement**-Creating an opinion about someone else is natural. People do it because of the inherent need for self-preservation as well as curiosity. It has a purpose, but there is a fine line that it can cross where it becomes counter intuitive. Avoid spending excessive amount of energy thinking about the actions of other people when they don't affect you.

37. **Reserve judgement**-Be alert so that you do not find yourself spending time to critique the actions of others based on how you believe you would have behaved or that person should have behaved. This action expends your energy in ways that are not fulfilling. Judgment does not serve you. It comes from a narrow-minded place that lacks understanding or compassion. You deserve understanding and compassion. If you cannot show it to others, you will not be able to show it to yourself.

38. **Outlets**-During challenging times everyone has their own coping mechanisms. Everyone choses an outlet for their feelings. Just because someone choses an outlet that is different than what you would choose does not mean they are less worthy of compassion. Likewise, if the outlet you chose during hard times was less productive than the outlet of someone else you should not feel that your value is diminished by your choices.

39. **Breaking points**- Everyone has a point that they run out of energy and willpower. People show it in different ways. When someone breaks it is often shown in the way they neglect other major facets of their lives. Do not worry about what is missing or incomplete from someone else's life. No one is perfect. In turn, do not get discouraged by what is missing from your life. Wholeness is a practice. It is a process and a state that varies.

40. **Overcoming judgement**-One of the most heavy weights you may carry is the opinions of others. Some people may not see you as who you are and desire to be. They may be stuck on who you were and things you did in the past. These opinions hold no value. Do not worry about the image other people may have of you when it does not match the image have for yourself. No one besides you knows who you are in your present state. They cannot read the thoughts that exist in your mind. They will not understand the vision that you have for yourself.

41. **Projections**-People commonly act based off their desires and what needs they want to fulfill. They may do this with no consideration of you and your needs or desires. This means that how people treat you has little to do with who you are. People behave toward you as a reflection of themselves. People who are rude, judgmental, or hurtful are doing this because they are motivated to behave that way due to a void that they are hoping to fill. They have unresolved emotions, and those behaviors are how they project them. People that treat you well and are open minded towards you do so because they come from a place of abundance that they wish to share with you.

42. **The self measuring tool**-If how you feel about yourself and how others feel about you does not matter then how do you measure yourself? Your behavior in the moment is the only indicator of who you are. The past is already gone, and the future has not occurred yet, so how you treat others and behave as each moment occurs is the only thing that reflects who you are and what you stand for.

43. **Don't worry about what others think**-No one will ever be able to form a 100% accurate picture of who you are, especially since people inherently are always changing. The ideas that people create about you are based off their limited life experiences and how they relate it to the limited experiences they have with you. Hoping to

control the image someone has of you is folly because humans are emotionally driven, and emotions are rarely reasonable. Your efforts will be rewarded more by focusing on how you treat others than if you expend energy to try influence what others think of you.

44. **False indicators of character-**When trying to form your self-perception it can be so hard to veer away from outside and negative influences. So, this is a reminder not to get caught up thinking about your past, what people remember you for, what you failed to succeed at and what you've been told you can't achieve. You are potential renews itself every moment and it is immeasurable.

Habits

45. **The journey of a thousand miles-**Its often said that the journey of a thousand miles begins with the first step. How you practice the steps in that journey determine where it takes you and how you get there. Your habits are what determine what the outcome of your life will be. This is both on a long and short term time frame. Your habits can be productive and propel you toward a high quality of life, or they can drive you further away from the life you desire. The composition of your habits decides your fate.

46. **Becoming aware-**Try to become conscious of what you are doing. If you frequently do something but you don't know why you do it, or what purpose it serves then chances are it's a habit. More accurately anything that you do over and over that does not align with your purpose and desires is a habit. There are a host of reasons that people create habits. People perform habits out of a desire for comfort. Perhaps because it does not require any extra thinking to do, or because they were raised or taught to behave in a certain way. Commonly it is because the habit actually is an outlet for that person under stress or confusion. If you want to obtain control

of your future take note of what habits you revert to, especially under pressure. Reshaping these subconscious actions is the key to directing your future.

47. **Unconscious habits**-You may not realize it but most of the actions you take are made up of your habits. If you unconsciously allow yourself to partake in self defeating activities such as negative self-talk and avoiding challenges, then when you are faced with adversity this will be your default response. But if you actively push yourself to step outside of your comfort zones and be open minded, then this will become your instinct. You will not even realize you are doing it because it has become who you are.

48. **Purposeful habits**-You can repetitively practice thoughts and actions to adopt them as habits. Reflect on what person you want to become. What habits is it going to take to get there? Make it a routine to reflect on this question and practice going through the motions of whatever those necessary habits are. In time it will become second nature and you will be on the way to having control over the course of your future.

Limiting Beliefs

49. **What are limiting beliefs**-It's time to come to terms with any idea in your head that is stopping you from achieving the life you want to live. These thoughts are limiting beliefs. It's that simple. Any negative idea that stops you from taking the steps you need to take to move toward your goals is a limiting belief. These beliefs are distractors. They cause you to stop before you even start. By better familiarizing yourself with what limiting beliefs are you can bypass them.

50. **False information from others**-Most of the information people get comes from other people. This does not mean the information is quality information. When passing information people will often speak from a place of theatrics because it fulfills the desire to be listened too. The naïve listener will believe these theatrics as a fact. A hill easily is seen as an impassable mountain due to this kind of communication. Do not allow yourself to be limited by the theatrical stories of other people. These stories hold little value or fact. They are not a good measure of the obstacles you will face or the unique path that you will walk.

51. **Limiting beliefs from past experiences**-Failure is frequently associated with pain. It carries a sort of trauma with it. People do what they can to avoid pain. Because of this when you fail at an any task it is easy become questioning of any future endeavor that is uncertain. You develop limiting beliefs to protect yourself from the pain of failure. This may cause you to try to talk yourself out from something before you can even start.

52. **When others fail**-If even one other person has done something then you can too. If no one has done it, you can be the first. People are always comparing themselves to others. They do it as a measure to compare progress. They may also do it as a way to plan for future actions. You cannot limit yourself to the results of someone else because you are not the same. Your drive is different, you approach is different, and your skills are different so your results will be different. So do not limit your ambition to someone else's results.

53. **The North Star**-It's important to have a guide against false beliefs and distractions that you will face. That guiding belief should be in your own ability. You have to believe that you "can." That you can access the same future as anyone else, and furthermore that you

can access outcomes that others have not achieved if you use the right tools.

Outlets

54. **Negative outlets**-Everyone has an outlet. A way to decompress after a long day. Something to look forward to every now and then. Some people are conscious of what their outlet is. Others do it instinctively, its practically a habit. Either way the important thing to consider is does your outlet rejuvenate you or is it only a distraction. Perhaps even another problem. Do you control your outlet, or does it control you and how does your outlet further effect your life?

55. **What is your outlet**-What do you find yourself craving or looking forward to? Every type of outlet has an appropriate frequency that is should be performed in. If you engage in some outlets as a regular occurrence it may add to your pain by becoming a distraction or creating new problems rather than relieving you of your troubles. So, pay attention to ensure you are using your outlet appropriately.

56. **The why of your outlet**-Whatever your outlet or outlets are you chose them for a reason. Try to understand why you picked whatever outlet you chose. This will point you in the direction to understanding what you may be hoping to escape from in your day to day life. An outlet should be balanced and rejuvenating. The point that it becomes an all out escape is when you need to ask yourself what you need to change about the life you are frequently trying to distract yourself from.

57. **The right outlet**-Find an outlet that doesn't control you, an outlet that doesn't run the risk of putting you in situations that can create more problems. Find an outlet that gives you a steady source of enjoyment and peace, rather than one that occasionally gives you

high doses of euphoria that leave you desperate and craving more of those "hits".

Recovering from trauma

58. **Restrained**-Take a moment to think about what the best version of yourself looks like. Is it someone who trusts more? Communicates better? Maybe you want to do a better job of setting boundaries? Whatever it is understand what that picture looks like. Now consider what is stopping you from behaving in that way? Your hesitation may come from pain that was created by trauma you have experienced. Unresolved trauma is a restraint. It will often come back to inhibit you unless you take a proactive approach to manage it.

59. **Shaming yourself**-One of the most common things keeping people from addressing their trauma is shame. The shame of what may have happened. Shame of how they may have acted or not acted. The shame of how they are being held back by it, and how it may make them feel to ask for help.

60. **Overcoming shame**-Whatever your traumatic experience was it does not define you. You do not have to be limited to whatever event occurred. How you survived, adapted to, or respond to the things that you endured is not something that you should feel ashamed of. You were doing the best you could with what you had, the same that anyone else would.

61. **Being trapped in your mind**- It's easy to feel guilty when you feel alone in your problems. Every problem is unique but the emotions and feelings surrounding them are shared by many other people. Open yourself up to the truth that you are not the only person to feel your emotions and make your mistakes. You have more in common

with people than you have different. Allow yourself to step back out into the world. Believe that no matter where you came from you can have the highest level of happiness possible. That you are equally deserving of peace than anyone else.

62. **Managing negative thoughts**-After trauma you will have uninvited negative thoughts occur. These thoughts will work to convince you that the worst possible outcome is going to occur and that it is too late to change it. When these thoughts occur, you must work to ground yourself in reality. You will often be your worst critic and hardest judge. Instead try to become your greatest supporter and caretaker.

63. **When trauma runs in the family**-Trauma coming from family and childhood is terrible. These are often some of your first relationships. The people you are supposed to be able to be the closest too. It can feel impossible to recover from the misconceptions created then because this is when you are most vulnerable. When your first and most consistent influences are negative it is hard to move forward. Despite how it seems the opinions and behaviors of family carries no extra significance from anyone else. Your family is human and flawed just like everyone else. The destructive things you saw or experienced from family still does not represent the rest of the world and all of the possibilities that exist.

64. **Relationship trauma**-Trauma caused by voluntary relationships is challenging because it can be hard to leave. When you volunteer your time and energy with other people it is hard to go against the judgment and effort that you have put in. When you make the decision to commit effort to someone its discomforting to think of turning away from a refuge that you thought you had. Relationships may dissolve for a number of reasons. It is not a reflection of you

worth or the future. It is a time to consider your conduct and how you may want to reorientate yourself as you move forward.

65. **Managing your triggers**-After a traumatic experience you may find yourself vulnerable to events that when they occur send you to a place of thoughts and emotions that are hard to manage. These are triggers. You owe it to yourself to pay attention to these triggers and find what they are. Understanding where these triggers come from gives you clues to find unresolved trauma that you may still need to recover from. By intercepting triggers, you empower yourself to have more control of your life and a deeper awareness of your emotions.

66. **Recovering from traumatic events**-The impact of a traumatic event will not disappear on its own. It requires devotion and time to overcome. It can be hard to revisit the most painful points of your life. It may feel easier to ignore it, but trauma cannot be hidden. Just like attempting to walk on a broken foot, living with a scarred mind will manifest itself in detrimental ways. It's vital to make an effort and practice of caring for your mind and digest events that you experience.

67. **Letting go of past pain**-Forward progress is almost impossible if you burden yourself down with negative feelings associated with the past. You have to relieve yourself of any destructive feelings you have towards yourself about the past.

68. **Feeling like you deserve to be punished**-Many people find themselves feeling like they deserved whatever events they endured. Others may feel like they deserve further punishment, or that punishment is a deserved result of some short coming they have. Punishment is destructive, it creates hesitation and hinders creativity. Accepting or believing you deserve substandard treatment you

will hold you back from the most energetic and productive version of who you can be.

69. **Trauma becomes an unconscious crutch**-Some people don't want to part ways with their trauma because of how it becomes a part of their identity. It becomes easier to brand themselves with a negative perception of who they are than fix it. Common examples are people who say things like "I'm an asshole." Or "I'm lazy." This is not who they are meant to be or their highest potential, but it is easier to state these things instead of dig deeper to find how to recreate themselves to not be "lazy" or "an asshole"

70. **Trauma affects your relationships**-After experiencing trauma you subconsciously may find yourself creating a defense so that you can avoid pain in the future. This defense may take the form of shortened or inappropriate communication. It may take the form of creating biased judgments towards other people. Regardless of how it manifests itself if it is not addressed it is going to hinder you from having fulfilling relationships. Be open minded when your around other people so that you can be aware of if your communication patterns and impressions are being influenced by trauma.

71. **Trauma affects the way you view yourself**-In traumatic events you often find that you felt helpless or like you had no control over what happened. This vulnerability can scar your identity and make you feel incapable and defenseless. Perhaps it may make you feel like a weak person. It is important to address these feelings, you had so that you may come to terms with your power and how you can have control in future situations. Getting that control back is critical to a full recovery.

72. **Perception of trauma**-Your mindset is important to your path to recovery. Certain experiences will leave you feeling like you are

powerless. You must be open to believing that you have the ability to achieve control of your life again. You can influence your future, and you can face he potentially traumatic situations that have occurred in the past and achieve a different result. You can still come out on top in life.

Setting boundaries

73. **Setting boundaries for yourself**-Setting boundaries allows you to create and control the space around you. Boundaries enable you to filter out the bad things and draw in the good. Only you know what is good for you, and what is not because no two peoples needs will completely mirror each other. Because of this it is your responsibility to set and understand what your boundaries are.

74. **Learning your boundaries**-Becoming aware of what your boundaries are will take time. Not all of the boundaries you create will be set in stone. Some may be flexible depending on where you are in life and what serves you at that time. You can begin to identify your boundaries by setting hard stops, these are things that have no purpose in your life under any circumstance. Things that are solely destructive. Identify things that hold no value to you, things that are only draining. This is where your hard boundaries should be. Next identify things that sometimes hold value to you. This is where your soft boundaries are. What you let in from this category will depend on where you are in life and what serves you at that time. Lastly identify things that always bring value to you. These are things that you will seek out and hope to draw towards you.

75. **Only you can truly value yourself and your time**-No one will better understand your desires than you. To achieve your desires and your highest quality of life you will have to proportionately employ your time and energy to achieve your preferred outcomes. You will

be the sole determinant of if you are moving in the direction you desire. You must have a high level of transparency with yourself to fill this role.

76. **Failing your boundaries**-If you find yourself having set a boundary for yourself that you can't seem to follow, this is a time to reflect inwardly. Does this boundary accurately represent what you are trying to accomplish? Is this boundary feasible? If not, what would it take to make this boundary more reasonable, but still effective? Do you need to develop a system that better enables you to have the discipline to follow up with your boundaries?

77. **Be mindful of your company**-You must be aware of who you allow into your life. There are some people who have no desire to acknowledge your boundaries. Some people only exist to serve themselves and will do anything to fulfill those desires regardless of who it negatively impacts. Be alert for signs that indicate someone is ready and willing to cross your boundaries, with no regard for how it will impact you.

78. **You don't owe anyone**-Not everyone will understand your desired trajectory. You may find that some people feel entitled to your time and energy. These people will not often return any of the effort that you give to them. At some point you have to assume responsibility of this situation. No one is entitled to any aspect of you. There are people who will continue to take from you until you have nothing left to give, not even to yourself. Do not allow yourself to become victim to this.

79. **Crossing boundaries**-When someone is not acknowledging your boundaries it is for one of two main reasons. They don't understand what your boundaries are, or they do not care. If you think the person crossing your boundaries is the first kind of person who is

simply unaware of what your boundary is, then it may you should explain what the boundary is and how it serves you. You are however, not obligated to explain why you have created a boundary. If you suspect the person does not care about your boundaries, then this likely reflects who they are as a person. Someone who does not care about your boundaries is so interested with what they desire that they are not concerned with how it may hurt you. This person is not someone who should hold space in your life.

80. **How to say no**-Ending communication with someone who drains your spirit can be a daunting task no matter how necessary it is. If you know your boundaries and someone is crossing them, you have to be firm in your resolve. You can take a wide range of approaches. Whether it involves limiting an aspect of your relationship with that person or cutting off your entire relationship with them entirely, be firm. It is nothing you should feel guilty for. If you are not the best version of yourself, you will not be able to give the best version of yourself to others. If someone hinders this progress, your decision to be without them is not an attack on them. It is a reflection of your love for yourself, and your commitment to the bigger picture.

81. **When to say no**-It's important to understand when to set a boundary for yourself. Boundaries should empower you by limiting harmful influences. In turn it should enable you to explore new possibilities. This is the purpose of boundaries. Ensure that the boundaries that are made to protect you do not begin to limit you.

Dealing with failure

82. **How to stop messing up all the time**-Do you feel like you're constantly making mistakes and wish it would stop? There is no one end all be all secret to make sure that you never fail again. You will always have moments where you fall short. You, like everyone else

in the world will never be perfect. However, what you can do is change your relationship to failure. You can turn failure into something that empowers you rather than debilitates you. That is what this next section is about.

83. **The concept of failure-**The idea of failure in itself is harmful and restrictive. It is seen as a dead end road. That there is no going back once you have failed at something. People view failure through fear, worried that it will forever be a stamp of who they are. This is wrong. Everyone fails, and everyone has fallen short. A person who pretends like they are without flaws is hiding. They are even missing out, and you'll learn why later. To start off, instead of thinking about failure as having to do with being wrong or incorrect, simply think of it as a being misguided.

84. **Failure as a guide-**As mentioned before its common to view shortcomings as an all-around failure. A dead end. You should change your relationship with your mistakes to one where you see them as an indicator of where you need to focus your attention. Then your failures become a guide for improvement and you in turn become unstoppable.

85. **Losses are a new opportunity-**Listen to your losses. Every time you lose another piece of a puzzle is found. Specifically, you are either being guided to or from something. Every loss has a lesson for you to learn from.

86. **The steppingstones to success-**Every person who seems complete or successful has only become so because of a series of failures that they learned form. This could be their own failures or someone else's but the hard lessons they learned from them are what created the foundation for a better life.

87. **Don't be afraid to fail-**Fear of failure holds many people back for their entire lives. Being afraid to be wrong traps people in a shell that sometimes feels impossible to break out of. Everyone fails. When you lose the shame associated with your shortcomings you propel yourself forward because you become comfortable with the discomfort of uncertainty. In time the process of trying, failing, and learning creates a wealth of knowledge that can be used to create the life you desire. But this path is only accessible to you accept that you will be imperfect.

88. **The misconception on failure-**Shame is a common feeling associated with failure, yet everyone has failed. Society has created a false standard for what success looks like by highlighting success and hiding failure. The reality is that failure happens much more frequently than success and its nothing to be ashamed of.

89. **Focus on the process-**Micromanaging the progress of your work can become an obsessive and unhealthy habit. Instead focus on how you do things not what the result is. Create a process that you think will lead to success and change the process as needed. Success without a process cannot be replicated but a process that is not initially successful can be changed and will become successful eventually. That process once successful can then be repeated to create more success.

90. **Ebbs and flows-**Imperfect times feel adverse because people are misled on how frequently hardship occurs. Hard times are common, they are natural, and they are part of life. Not every moment, day, week, month, or year is going to be great. Life ebbs and flows. Resisting it makes it much more painful. Accepting it puts you back in control. It allows you to enjoy what the moment is rather that what you are trying to force it to be.

91. **When failure inspires**-In closing failure will mold or break people. It is critical to become comfortable with it. It's not an option but a necessity because failure will always exist. Changing your relationship to failure will change your relationship with the rest of your life because of how it will relieve you off false beliefs associated with success and inspire you to put exert yourself authentically.

Rejection

92. **Rejection is a form of communication**-There are hard rejections and soft rejections. You will receive a hard rejection when you present an idea that someone feels holds an empty or negative outcome to them. This will generally be displayed by a firm "No" or a continuous string of more soft diverting tactics, such as changing the subject or avoiding answering your question. A soft rejection is how someone responds when your idea does not currently hold value but has the potential to hold value under different terms or at a different time. You will receive more of a back-and-forth communication with them some indicator that the terms of your proposal would be satisfactory if revised or presented at a later date.

93. **Rejection is a form of bargaining**-Do not attempt to disrespect someone by crossing a hard boundary. When you encounter a soft boundary, this is a time to listen and understand the desires of the person you are communicating with. Regardless both boundaries are a form of communication. How people respond to your boundaries and how you respond to other people's boundaries is a way of understanding how to interact with others, and who you should interact with. The back and forth communication of these ideas is like bargaining. You will either come to accept common ideas and goals or you will find that your ideas and goals do not support each other.

94. **Compromise, to not compromise**-When a relationship ends between two people it often becomes a sensitive and personal event. Both parties receive the end of the relationship as an attack on them. It's not. It is a declaration that the commitment to communication and company no longer hold value. That the objective and interests of the parties are different and to pretend like they are not would require more energy than to let them go. It is not a negative thing. It is a time to reflect on your performance in how you behave towards others. It is also a opportunity to save and redirect your energy towards what brings you energy in return.

95. **Rejection is not a reflection of your character**-Understand above all that rejection is not a mark on you character, value or progress. If you were rejected it does not diminish your value. If your ideas were rejected it does not mean that they are wrong. You just have to find where you and your ideas will be appreciated, or how to present them in ways that they can be better understood.

96. **Rejection is not terminal**-Rejection is felt most heavily when someone does not take in perspective how miniscule it is in comparison to limitless possibilities that exist. Rejection by one person or group of people is not a reflection of the responses that will be received by other people or groups. Rejection during one period of life does not entail rejection for the duration of life. Rejection is an active form of communication and like failure is a steppingstone to greater things.

Comfort Zones

97. **What are comfort zones**-If you cannot remember the last time you've felt uncomfortable or challenged then you are likely intimately familiar with comfort zones. Comfort zones are

psychological barriers that stop you from having to ask yourself questions about yourself and the world around you.

98. **Why to leave your comfort zones**-If you are not actively molding yourself and your life then it will mold you. The constant influx of things you are exposed to is too dynamic to maintain a stagnant position. You will be driven to change unconsciously if you do not make a conscious effort to focus on who you want to be. This is why it is important to leave your comfort zones. When you leave your comfort zones you become more aware of yourself and how you want to fit into the world.

99. **How to leave your comfort zones**-Leaving your comfort zones is more simple than people make it out to be. You don't have to trek through the desert for a week to be outside of your comfort zones. Simply allow yourself to be around ideas and settings that challenge you to examine your beliefs and systems. Try to choose things that align with where you desire to be. Do not do anything that is against your hard boundaries or that may not be safe.

100. **Keep comfortable spaces**-Leaving your comfort zones is vitally important. When your life is dictated by comfort zones, you need to take action. That in mind, you don't have to leave every thing that is comfortable in your life, and you should have places and moments that provide you care and comfort. You should have balance. Its important to have moments where you can recharge, and commune in a safe and trusted environment.

When things get hard

101. **Lean into your purpose**-When things get crazy around you it can be hard to make sense of it all. You may find greater peace by making sense of who you are and where you fit into the grand scheme

of things. Who you are at your core should remain consistent. This refers to your values and purpose. When things get hard lean into this to find direction.

102. **Reflect on what you can control**-When you aren't sure what you can control take a step back and take note of what you can control. This will help you feel centered, and you can use this point as a foot hold to move forward to finding and influencing things other aspects that you did not feel you can control.

103. **Focus on your goals**-When you're facing a challenging period in life you may feel like you don't know where to start in order to begin getting your life back in order. Identify goals that you feel will help you get you through your hardship. You can focus on these goals and use them as a grounding point when you when you feel lost. Keep in mind it doesn't have to be anything extravagant. Even setting simple goals like making a good meal or working out will be a good start as you establish your grounding.

Quitting

104. **Responding to pressure**-Pressure is like a fire that will either mold and strengthen your mind or melt away your resolve. You have the option to choose which of these outcomes will happen. You do this by determining what your response to pressure will be before you encounter it. Understand and accept the obstacles you will face before they happen. Don't worry about if you will be able to overcome them or what you will do when you encounter them, instead decide what you will do beforehand so that you can use adversity to shape you rather than break you.

105. **Is quitting bad**-Although it is a productive practice to commit to overcoming adversity there are people who will commit so heavily

to this practice that by the time they achieve their objective it has costs them more than they will ever gain from it. Sometimes they may never achieve their objective. Because of this there is an appropriate time and place to terminate your efforts to a commitment.

106. **Don't always just "Keep trying"**-Some people are driven by a mantra of "never give up." Or "don't quit." This can be in regard to jobs, relationships, or any number of activities. The problem with this mantra is it breeds an environment of blind will and close mindedness. If you do not stop to reevaluate your goal and your actions to achieve said goals, you may find yourself figuratively trying to dig through a concrete wall when you could have gone around it or were not made to go through it in the first place.

107. **When to try again**-If the process of what it takes to do something is consistent, such as the time and energy cost are the same, but your motivation wanes, it is not appropriate to quit yet. You can access if your goal still carries the same value to you. But if the only thing that has changes is that you have become discouraged its not appropriate to throw your work and desires out the door. It's time to take a break, reassess your approach, and continue on.

108. **When to quit**-Every action you take should serve you in one way or another. Your lack of action at times may serve you more than your actions. When you commit to a goal you should do so because you have a full understanding of what it will take to accomplish that goal, why you want to accomplish the goal, and what value accomplishing that goal will bring to you. You should frequently reexamine these three factors throughout your pursuit. If the time comes where one of these three things drastically changes, and the original picture is no longer the same then it is time to either reconsider your approach or what priority this goal will take or quit the goal all together.

109. **The Timeframe of Success**-The compound effect of steadily gaining experience at something almost ensures that in time a person will achieve some form of success. If you have a goal that is truly important to you, have the patience to practice it consistently through its struggles and the experience you gain over time will practically ensure some success. The problem is that often people view success in a narrow time frame. As time wears on and they don't feel any closer they consider that they may have "failed" and that they should consider quitting. When the reality is success is coming, just not in the time that they desired.

Moving forward

110. **Misconceptions**-As you attempt to move forward and mold yourself into who you want to be you will find yourself dealing with many misconceptions you may have about yourself. These misconceptions were created traumatic experiences you have had, and they will limit you from accessing the best version of yourself. This section covers some of those misconceptions and how you may overcome them.

111. **You're not weird**-you may have been made to feel that your interests or behaviors make you to be the odd person out. This is untrue. Everyone has unique interests and unusual habits, but not everyone expresses them. If you are surrounded with authentic people, they will reveal these things to you. People who are not brave enough to be authentic may lash out at you as a form of defense because they are upset that they do not live as the most authentic version of themselves.

112. **You're not alone**-It may feel like your journey or feelings are so unique that no one else can understand what you're going through. Though everyone's story is unique, many occurrences and feelings

are common among other people. Not enough people express these things, so as a result it's easy to feel isolated. When you open up in the right way to the right people, others will be inspired by your transparency, and they may also reveal their struggles. You will find many to be more similar than you would expect.

113. **You can be accepted**-You may have been victimized in the past and made to feel that you are not deserving of love or do not have the ability to fit in with others, but you can. The people who tore you down are not what define you or your future. You have a place in the world, and with others.

114. **You are not defined by an event**-Sometimes you may feel labelled by an event that has occurred in your life. You may feel like you are boxed in by whatever happened and that your future is limited. But you are not. The future has unlimited possibilities, and you have unlimited potential. These possibilities begin with you looking past what has occurred in the past and enabling yourself to achieve your desires.

115. **You choose what you are known for**-You are the decider of your reputation. Your reputation will be divided into two main aspects. First is how you make others feel. It doesn't matter how skilled you are if you constantly draw away from the energy of others. Secondly, is what you chose to project yourself as. You can highlight the best qualities of yourself and make them the focal point of what others see in you.

116. **You are equal to others**-Certain negative experiences and abusive people may have led you to believe that for whatever reason you are not of the same value as others. But you are. Think to before you encountered the harmful experiences that you did, about who you were. The wholeness that you felt. That is the wholeness that has

always existed within you, but you were misguided to a point that left you lost and unable to understand your worth.

117. **Your interests and desires matter**-Because you matter, your interests and desires matter. There is a time and a place to put yourself second but make sure that you are not always taking the back seat to the pursuits of other people. You deserve to spend your life and time experiencing the things that your soul desires.

118. **Your value**-Your worth will never be changed. All people have the same inherent worth as others. What can change is the value you that you provide people. Some people spend time and energy draining from others and only thinking about themselves. Others lead a life of abundance where they contribute to the happiness and wellbeing of those around them.

119. **You can't**-You may have the idea that you can't do something. That certain opportunities that are accessible to other people are not accessible to you. You may believe you are underserving, don't have the skill, or a variety of other intrusive thoughts. This is false. You can. You can do anything else that someone else has done and you can be the first to do something new. You just need to find out how. That is the only thing separating you from your goals.

Friction

120. **The Fog**-Living the life you want should be simple. But friction occurs to move you away from the path you set by challenging you and testing your understanding of things that you thought you knew. Friction is the emotions and events that occur to make what should be simple complex. These are the things you must be prepared for and understand to maintain integrity to yourself and your goals.

121. **Failed expectations**-Throughout your journey you are going to create expectations for yourself or other people. These expectations are not always going to be met. It will be up to you to respond to these events in a manner that serves you and further encourages yourself and those around you.

122. **Your response to failed expectations**-Sadness, hopelessness, and anger are all different ways you may want to respond in the presence of failed expectations. These are natural responses to this event. Take the time to digest those emotions. Also, when you find yourself carrying these negative emotions but don't know why examine your past and consider if these feelings are due to expectations that you carried that were not met.

123. **The uncertain future**-You may at times find yourself plagued with anxiety. Even when you are able to hold it from your thoughts it may be at the back of your mind. It will manifest itself in atypical ways. If you find yourself doing destructive things that you do not have a reason for, consider if your actions may be a coping mechanism for unresolved anxiety.

124. **Coping with uncertainty**-There are many outlets for anxiety today. The most important thing is that you find one. Eliminating anxiety will help you stay present so that you are getting the most out of every moment. It will help you experience the present rather than becoming caught in the future.

125. **Unresolved trauma**-After experiencing trauma that you have been unable to resolve you may find yourself having dramatic and unpredictable changes in your moods. Bursts of anger, erupting in tears, depression, or solemness are a few but not all of ways that your unresolved trauma may be manifesting itself.

126. **Managing unresolved trauma**-After you have experienced an outburst reflect on if the triggering factor warranted the response you demonstrated. If it seems disproportionate, consider if your outbursts may be related to something else. Something from the past. If you suspect this take the time and resources to treat the underlying source of your emotional swings.

127. **Overworking**-If your mind is constantly occupied you may never have adequate time to digest trauma that you experience throughout your life. You may in fact be using work as a way to avoid these traumas. If the work, you exert does not have a definitive objective then you may be using work as a distractor. This is unhealthy in the long term as you will eventually have to come face to face with the things you may have done or felt.

128. **Finding balance**-Make it a priority in your life to set aside time to relax. Set aside a separate time to reflect on your future and past. This will enable you to move forward rested and clear about why you do what you do.

129. **Understanding fear**-Fear comes from lack of understanding. Fear is often perpetuated by stories of mishaps that other people have experienced. Fear breeds hesitation and promotes stagnation.

130. **Get educated**-Educate yourself on things that scare you. This way you may know how to avoid them or overcome them if that is what the solution you must take.

131. **Emotional management**-Emotional management is important because it is what enables you to get the highest quality experiences. Emotional management is the key to putting you in the driver's seat of your life. If your emotions are unmanaged and control you then you are not going to be able to show up as the best version

of yourself and in turn you are not going to be able to receive the highest value out of the opportunities, you are given.

132. **Unresolved emotions**-Unresolved emotions will weigh you down in a variety of ways. Every event that occurs that is held onto in a negative way will manifest itself in ways that you may not intend for them too. For this reason, it is important to make sure that your pain is not left unresolved, but do not become so set in solving every problem that you become trapped in this endeavor. It will be a practice that will provide solutions in time.

133. **Projected emotions**-You may find yourself displaying emotions that are disproportionate to the events that seem cause them. This is often because you are projecting your emotions from past events onto current events. On the same note you may feel negative emotions during times that should be neutral or positive as a projection of unresolved emotions. In other words, your projected emotions will not always be during high stress events. They may occur during low stress events because of unresolved stress.

134. **Take a moment**-Society throws so much at people that they are constantly having to interact with a new stimulus. You don't. It's okay to take a moment or longer to step away from events that trigger you or that you are not ready for. It's okay to gather your thoughts so that when you express yourself you are doing so in a way that best represents you.

135. **Emotional Control**-Not every situation warrants an immediate reaction, or an action in general. If you are constantly reacting to every situation then you are allowing your environment to form you rather than maintaining control and forming your environment to support your life and needs.

136. **The emotional reaction**-Though not every situation warrants a reaction it is important to express yourself. It's a natural part of being a human. Don't be so focused on managing your emotions that you never speak your truth. Don't be so focused on managing your emotions that you're afraid to be in the moment and blissfully enjoy life.

B. Finding your power

After providing yourself with the gifts of internal peace it's time to look externally. It's time to decide what you want to create in the world. Its time to decide your purpose and how you will accomplish it to have the greatest impact on the world around you.

Recreating yourself

137. **Why Change**-Once you have found peace you will likely look around and see that the life you've been living, and who you are was a product of the chaos and uncertainty that you were facing. You deserve to experience a version of life that is not a reflection of this turmoil. You may wonder how to even go about making those changes in your life. This chapter poses some thoughts to consider so that you can orient yourself to a person that is guided by control and purpose.

138. **Who are you**- "Who are you?" This is not only a question of identity but also a declaration of action. "Who you are" is not only about what you feel, but also about what you will do. This is the idea of how you view the world, how you fit into it, and how you will influence it.

139. **What are your values**-Your values are the concepts that you want to represent as you live. They are the pillars that you will base your

actions on. Not everyone's values will be the same. You don't need to have a million different descriptions either. But your values should serve as a baseline for how to behave.

140. **Stay in touch with yourself**-Before you enter your day and even consider how you will form the world around you, you need to take note of how you are treating yourself. Make sure your self-perception is on track and is one that enables you to achieve your desires.

141. **Check your beliefs.** -After examining your relationship to yourself you need to examine how you believe you can impact the world around you. Examine the language you are using to describe your day, your goals, and your outlook in general. This new outlook should be one that is no longer limited by negative beliefs that were created from past traumatic experiences.

142. **What do you stand for**-Before you leave your bed and come in contact with anyone else you must decide what you stand for. What standards are you going to hold? These standards are going to serve as a guide for what you want to strive toward but also what you refuse to accept from the world around you. These standards are going to be a reference for how you pick your boundaries and community.

143. **Visualize your influence**-If you want to have the best impact possible, you have to decide how you will impact others. Decide how you will use your standards and values together to project positivity and be a creator. Keep in your mind, an idea of what people should take away after interacting with you, and how they should feel.

144. **You will impact the world**-Regardless of how you plan your day, or what you do or don't embody keep in mind that you will have

an impact on the world. It is simply up to you what you want that impact to be, and what how far it reaches.

145. **You're not made to fit into a box**-Normalcy is a subjective standard that varies from person to person. So do not try to "fit in" to anyone else's idea of what you are meant to be. Don't be afraid to be creative and step outside of what isn't commonly seen. You decide who you want to be and make that happen. Don't limit your growth to anyone else's standards or lack of.

The New You

146. **Finding your power**-Come to terms with the power that you have over your life and acknowledge the responsibility that you have, to use your energy to mold your environment to create the life that best serves you. This section has some guidelines to consider as you find your footing.

147. **You Deserve You**-Though there are many reasons to recreate yourself do it most of all because you deserve the best version of yourself. You deserve the experience you will get from this.

148. **Finding your new identity**-After you have shed negative misconceptions you had about yourself you will develop a new outlook on who you are. This outlook will be fluid, as you grow and change. You should have an image of how you will present yourself and behave. This is when you decide what you want out of life as well. You have the power to create your outcome and experience.

149. **Don't wait to be the best version of yourself**-It can be nerve wracking but don't wait to dedicate yourself to making the transition to empowerment. It will not happen overnight. It may have some hiccups, but it will be worth it.

150. **Go first-**It can be nerve wracking to transition from whatever actions and behaviors you've been doing, especially when you're the first one. But you owe it to yourself. The right people will be drawn to you rather than feel threatened by you. This initiative will give you more information about your environment and how you may need to change it.

151. **Give value to those around you-**As you become more empowered, do not become judgmental or cynical. This is an opportunity to inspire others through your actions and growth.

152. **Do not be dampened-**People may question or even discourage you. Prepare yourself for this and keep in mind that throughout your transition other people may find themselves in violation of your boundaries. Not everyone is going support you, but their lack of support is not a reflection of you or the path that you should take, so do not allow yourself to be discouraged.

153. **Don't look to others for approval-**If you look to others for approval, you will constantly be held back. Whether you desire to lead others or not leading your own life is the quality of a leader. This is a quality you must adopt in order to achieve progress for yourself. If you are constantly questioning what others think you will be taking a step backwards for every step forwards.

154. **How will you make others feel-**How you make others around you feel, will have a direct impact on your experience. If you open yourself up to others in a kind way, they will be drawn to you and encourage or even enable you. If you close yourself off and treat others in rude ways you will be shunned, and future doors will be closed before they could ever be opened.

155. **Shine your light**-Your energy, experience, and perceptions are unique from everyone else in the world. Therefore, it will always have value. Don't ever be afraid to shine your light on others because someone somewhere needs to hear what you have to share.

156. **Hold your space**-As you find yourself moving to new levels you may feel a bit of imposter syndrome. Anyone who has been in your shoes or higher has felt this. Hold on through the storm and in time these feelings will pass. But if you quit because of your apprehensions then you will never fill the shoes that you deserve to be in.

157. **You belong where you desire to be**-You will not go where you desire to be if you do not envision yourself there and act like you belong to be there. Orientate your mind towards your goals and you will subconsciously take the steps to arrive there. If you do not take these steps your journey will be much more challenging.

158. **Removing your ego**-Taking your ego out of the picture is important because an untrained ego can cause many distracting thoughts. The ego obsesses with accomplishment. Plan for what you need to do to achieve your goals. Allow your progression to be your indicator of success and not what your ego is feeling.

159. **Misconceptions about power**-Power comes internally rather than externally. Some believe power is an exercise of control over others, but it should be reflection of control over yourself. The greatest reflection of power may appear externally because of how the control you have over yourself enables you to understand and impact the world.

160. **You are limitless**-You have the ability to be anywhere, doing anything that you desire. It is simply a matter of taking the steps to get there.

Express your authentic self

161. **Expressing your truth**-The idea of genuinely displaying one's desires and interests can feel daunting in the face of a world that judges quickly and lacks transparency. People are so afraid expressing their truth that some lash out at those who do, because they are envious of that vulnerability. Others are waiting for someone to set that example. They are waiting for that inspiration. So, your truth may not appeal to everyone but those that it does appeal to are the people you deserve to be around and will in turn add value to your life.

162. **Displaying your gift**-Everyone has a gift. A talent, that they are passionate about. You deserve to give yourself the opportunity to explore the extent of this talent. It doesn't have to be something that will gain you the attention of the world or make you rich overnight. Your talent is simply something that you feel genuine enjoyment out of doing that you can share with others.

163. **How to stand out**-Standing out is not about flexing your power, it is about helping other people understand theirs. When you make others feel elevated and encourage them to be the highest version of themselves you will not be forgotten.

164. **The best version of yourself**-The best version of a person is in line with their purpose, in touch with their truth and knows how to express themselves appropriately. The best version of you doesn't have to compare with or be better than anyone else.

Life's purpose

165. **Does it exist**-People often become fixated on the question of if life has a grand purpose. They look to many different sources to

uncover or understand what this purpose may be so that they can have a guide to live by. Any guide ever found by someone only serves as a template that still must be interpreted. At the end of the day all those who feel they have purpose are creating that purpose, by interpreting whatever template they have chosen. You have the ability to create your purpose around whatever you deem worthy.

166. **How to find it-**You will find the ideas to create your purpose from your values and talents. A life driven by these things will feel natural and fulfilling because it is living as reflection of what you what to create in the world. Not everyone's purpose and ideas will be the same. No one person's purpose is higher than others, they are all equally valuable no matter how different.

167. **How to live it-**To live your life's purpose you must have the courage to be different. You must take the initiative to follow whatever set of ideas you have chosen for yourself. You will need to turn your beliefs into a regular practice, because you will not always be in line with them. You will need to frequently reflect on if you are in line with your purpose. A life with purpose becomes a journey instead of a destination because it is a set of values and actions that is so powerful it is worthy of living for. Instead of sifting from desire to desire or accomplishment to accomplishment you can be grounded in you ever consistent purpose.

Communication

168. **The importance of communication-**One of the barriers to happiness in life is poor communication. If you communicate inappropriately your relationships, goals, and overall experience in life will suffer. Learning to communicate in a way that others can relate to will greatly improve your experience in life.

169. **The world is "your team."**-The foundation of good communication begins with changing how you view those that you are communicating with. Communication can be daunting at times, if you change the picture of communication to one where you are working with everyone to achieve a common goal rather than possibly against them it gives you an edge in communication.

170. **The perspective of others**-When you understand the perspective of others you are taking the first step to opening yourself up to adding them to your team. By taking the time to understand what they hope to gain out of an interaction you're putting their needs first, enabling them to see you as team mate rather than a potential threat.

171. **Helping others understand your perspective**-When the time comes for you to state your side of the interaction its most effective to do it with "I" statements. Convey how you are feeling in a practical human, way that they can understand too. Avoid statements that may be taken as an attack that can cause the other person to feel cornered.

172. **Rule of reciprocation**-You have the opportunity to set the tone and pace of every interaction you have based off of your actions. Keep in mind that your behavior is a communication tool that sets the example for what kind of treatment you are hoping to receive during your interaction. If someone else takes initiative to set the interaction in a negative way do not take it personal. This is a form of communication for you to listen to.

173. **Communication through feeling**-Successful communication is not only evaluated on what is said but also what is felt. If you went into a very hard subject but made the other person, feel valued and understood, then the next time you have to communicate on a

hard subject they will be receptive to you. But if you go into an easy subject and make the other person, feel terrible, they will remember that and not even want to talk to you about easy problems.

174. **Your long term evaluation**-One good interaction is not going to win you the hearts and minds of the entire world, just like one imperfect interaction is not going to ruin it for you. You are being evaluated by others on the compilation of how you make others around you feel, throughout time on a long-term basis.

175. **Active listening**-The most important part of communication is listening. Before you even think about what you have to say ensure that you have listened and understand what the other party is trying to say. If they have said everything you feel is important continue to listen so that they can know that they are understood, and you are a safe place to come to for their expression.

Independence

176. **Building self-reliance**-Building the life that you want takes a certain level of self-reliance. This is a skill that must be practiced and learned. It enables you to face the future. By no longer being reliant on outside sources you will have the courage to ask the questions needed that will help you solve the problems that are holding you back.

177. **Finding solutions**-you must practice finding solutions. If you are stopped in your tracks at every obstacle you encounter your progress will be slow. Learning to find your own solutions or develop a system that helps you find solutions keeps you moving forward with less stress and idle time.

178. **Take it a step at a time**-If you have spent most of your life reliant upon others it will likely take time to create a life separate from co-dependency. Start with accomplishing simple tasks, and in time your ability to be intuitive will increase and you will find yourself taking on bigger tasks and reaching new heights.

179. **Self-accountability**-The most important aspect of self-reliance is self-accountability. You have to honestly be able to reflect on your progress and decide if it is adequate or how you need to make improvements to your process.

A winning mentality

180. **The mental game**-The mentality you approach the world with has a direct impact on your durability and success. Choosing to be optimistic and flexible will put you a step ahead of whatever you face. The following thought processes are those of someone who plans to win against whatever they face.

181. **Lead your life**-You have to lead the life you want to life. It will not magically appear. You must focus your energy on what you want to create and take the initiative to create it.

182. **Empowering yourself**-The way you talk, think, and act are all inter-connected. Behaving negatively in one of these ways will always transfer over. If you talk positively, you will enable yourself to think positively and in turn empower yourself to act in a positive manner.

183. **Act like a host**-When you're new somewhere don't sit in the shadows and hope to have a good experience. Take initiative. Act almost as if you are one of the hosts and it's your job to create a good experience for those around you. This will draw others to you and facilitate a great experience for you as well as those around you.

184. **Approve yourself-**If you wait for other people to encourage you and approve of your ideas before you make a move, you're going to be limited to the minds of others. It's possible the people you're taking advice from may not think as big as you either. If you want to build true momentum you should be willing to act without approval beforehand.

185. **You are significant-**Every moment that passes becomes a part of history. It becomes part of someone's memory forever. So don't question your significance. Every time you interact with someone you are impacting them in some way. The question is how do you intend to influence the people you interact with?

186. **Leading your day-**Develop a purpose for your day. Even if that purpose is just to relax. Waking up with a distinct purpose in mind gives you the ability to guide the way that your every day will go.

187. **Sculpting your mind-**Decide what your mentality will be when you wake up and take time to reflect on it throughout the day. By fostering a strong mentality, you give yourself the opportunity to create the energy needed to create the outcome you desire. If your plan is like the steering wheel for your day, then your mentality is the gas for the vehicle.

Abundance and scarcity

188. **Abundance versus scarcity mentality-**There are two ways to view the world. The first is through the lenses of scarcity. This is the idea that anything good that happens is a rarity and that there is only a limited amount of opportunity in the world. The second is through abundance. The idea that life is filled with opportunities and that good things are a result of living in the right way.

189. **Abundance**-Changing your outlook to one where you see the abundance of the world relieves you of stress. It gives you courage to be selective with your energy. The best part is that believing in abundance will encourage you to create abundance.

190. **You are scarce**-The true scarcity in the world is you. There is only one of you, and you only have one life to live. You have the ability to walk many paths but not every path is made for you to walk.

191. **No opportunity is missed**-Because you are a form of abundance in the world, no opportunity alone is so exceptional that it cannot be found or created again. Because of this you should never sacrifice your standards over the concern of "missing out."

192. **Think in possibilities**-Do not stress about missed opportunities. Be excited about the unlimited possibilities and experiences that you have not yet had the pleasure of having.

193. **Finding possibilities**-Limitless possibilities exist for you, but you must poise yourself to receive them. You must open your mind to be creative when entering new environments and meeting new people to opportunities that align with your purpose and desires. Be flexible, to consider things that you have not experienced and be open to reconsidering things that you thought you already knew, so that opportunities may present themselves to you.

194. **Know what your cost is**-Develop a sense of importance regarding your time and energy. You should have a mental indicator for when something uses a disproportionate amount of your energy or time. Incorporate this into your boundaries and use it as a measure of how adequately something serves you.

195. **Know what you bring to the table**-Have standards for yourself. Know what unique value and skillsets you carry with you. Ensure that you are being used to your highest and best potential, don't ever let anything limit you from doing this.

196. **The Peak of Abundance**-The highest form of abundance is when people and opportunity are drawn to you. At this point you will no longer have to search for abundance because it finds you. This will only be the result of a balance and energetic life. A life where you are in line with your boundaries but equally in touch with your purpose. As you live with passion, others will feel drawn to your energy, to support you and grow with you.

C. The Practice

Nothing is ever mastered overnight and anything that is perceived to be mastered will take a consistent repetition to stay proficient at. Managing your emotions are behaviors are no different. Everything in the previous sections will need to be a practice but the parts going forward deserve extra care.

Relationships

197. **Defining relationships**-A relationship is an unspoken set of expectations between two people. Ideally it is mutually beneficial but at the least it should be neutral. Pay attention to how your relationships use your time and energy.

198. **Relationships are not made to complete you**- When you come from a history of trauma you may find yourself doubting your worth. A common behavior of people with this history is the desire of hoping to find a relationship that can give them back aspects of themselves that they have lost. This is a dangerous idea for both you and your relationship. Only you can do the work to heal yourself.

The best relationships are made of two complete people who make a conscious effort to care both for themselves individually and the relationship. You should not enter a relationship hoping that someone will do your growth for you. This action of creating co-dependency can have troublesome consequences.

199. **Not every relationship is worth having**-Its not uncommon to visualize what an ideal relationship looks like to you. This can even be a good practice. But be warry of trying to fit something in a mold that it is not made to go in. Not everyone shares the same vision of the relationship they want, and the same kind of relationship isn't suited for every person. You may find that after time of working to have someone's attention, or to make a relationship fit into a certain cast, that it is not worth the time and energy you have put forth. You can put yourself in danger of spending infinite amounts of time and energy to never achieve your desired result.

200. **Not all love is equal**-You may unfortunately come to the finding's that the attention that a person gave to someone else is not the same amount of attention that they will give you. This is often unintended and unrealized, but it happens. Know what you will accept for yourself from others, if someone is not able to give the communication and attention that you desire then do not be afraid to walk away and find spaces where you can have what serves you.

201. **Evading the negativity of others**-No one is 100% positive all of the time. Do not discount people because they say negative things sometimes but pay attention to when a person has more negative to say than positive. Their outlook on the world with influence yours.

202. **Have conscious relationships**-When you're in a relationship it is important to take conscious steps to ensure its success. It is important to have regular communication to ensure that your

relationship is fulfilling and meeting any expectations you and the other involved parties may have set.

203. **Love is patient**-A relationship requires patience. It requires the understanding that no one is perfect and that the involved parties will not always meet the standards that you desire, the same way you will not always meet what they desire. It's important to be patient and communicate clearly when your expectations are not met. It is equally as important to listen to how the other person feels about your desires or expectations of them.

204. **Love is empathetic**-Understand that your relationships do not exist with the sole purpose of serving you. They are not all about you. A good relationship will have a give and take dynamic. All parties will sometimes have to put the success of the relationship above their immediate interests. In turn the right relationship will return that value to the involved parties.

205. **Know your partner**-It is important to devote time and interest to your partner as they should to you. Understand them. What motivates them, what worries them, and everything in between. Understand what they desire out of life so you can consider how to help create that picture with them.

206. **Understand your partner**-Make an effort to understand your partner's perspective. When you find yourself experiencing friction try to take a moment to understand where your partner is coming from. Reflect on why they may have a certain perspective. Only once you've taken time to understand their view are you in the position to consider how to present your views in a way that they can understand.

207. **Love communicates**-This section encompasses a lot of different ideas. None of them are possible without communication. Communication in your relationships is key. Too often people assume someone should know what they are thinking. No two people's minds are gong to be the exact same because the events that form how people think are never the exact same from person to person. You could have the same desires as someone and not know it if you don't communicate, you could also be allowing a small problem to destroy a relationship that would be an easy fix with communication.

208. **When to end a relationship**-When a relationship begins to draw more from you than it gives you it is time to reassess that relationship. Maybe it's a miscommunication and a conversation is all that is needed to fix it, or maybe it is time for that relationship to come to an end.

209. **Enjoy the journey of a relationship**-Every relationship is going to have its ups and downs, they will have storms you have to weather. But if your involved with the right people, your relationships will propel you. They will add joy to your life and present new avenues and opportunities. Enjoy the journey that comes from your relationships.

Productivity

210. **Understanding patterns of success or failure**-Have you ever noticed that people who are successful at one thing tend to be successful at many other things? That is because success and failure are determined by the patterns and habits you create. The actions used to be successful at one endeavor can be mirrored to be successful at a different task. On the same note the habits that lead people off the

course of success in one aspect of their life will likely do the same in other aspects of their life.

211. **Patterns of failure-**There are behaviors that doubtlessly will lead one away from their desires rather than too them. Patterns such as being controlled by doubt, being limited by comfort, and accepting unsatisfactory results from yourself. Strict patterns of failure are those that limit you from challenging yourself and asking questions that cause you to grow.

212. **Find time to relax-**As you develop your plan to achieve the life you want set aside time to relax. It's important to set time aside to clear your mind and enjoy yourself or all the work you are doing will feel pointless. Reaching your goals may require vast amounts of effort. Approaching your goals relaxed and with the right frame of mind enables the work you exert to take you further when you are in a fresh and open state of mind.

213. **Starting small-**Creating the life of your dreams isn't only about getting the big decisions right and that isn't what creates a successful process. It begins with the smaller habits that will compound to give you power over the big moments. Small things like the mentality that you face the day with, and your planning process are what will help you reach success.

214. **Making each moment count-**Every moment is important and has a purpose. Don't stress on over establishing the purpose of every moment but simply understand that it has a purpose and be okay with whatever the purpose of that moment is. The purpose of one moment may be locking down an incredible deal while the purpose of another may be waiting in line for an appointment. Each of those purposes is important and facilitates the overall happiness and success of your life.

215. **View time in sections**-One way that you can help establish small goals and give yourself the satisfaction of feeling productive is by dividing your goals into sections. You could establish that your goal for the morning is simply to work out and your goal for the whole week is to read a book. Doing this will help rid you of the annoying and lingering feeling that there is something that you are supposed to be doing.

216. **Set a pattern of success**-Success and failure are determined by unconscious habits. So, ask yourself what are you doing when you don't realize you're doing it, and where does that take you? Have you created an unconscious habit of failing to plan or perhaps the opposite where you have now become what seems to be a natural planner? Which one do you think will serve you best?

217. **Stopping destructive habits**-The first step to creating good habits is stopping bad habits. Don't feel like you are behind the curve because you aren't waking up at 4am, working out, and making a healthy breakfast when in fact simply waking up before 9am instead of 12pm is an accomplishment and a step in the right direction.

218. **The trap of comfort**-The biggest limit you can impose upon yourself is to be guided by comfort. If you demand that every step of your journey, be comfortable you will not make it far, and you may not be happy. Humans crave external stimulus. A life driven by comfort may feel good, but you will in time find that it lacks any stimulation to fuel your soul. Not every step of your journey should be like walking on smoldering rocks through freezing rain but if discomfort is a wall for you, then your productivity will be limited.

219. **Finding new habits**-Finding the right habits for you is a matter of finding where you want to be or what processes you need to adopt

to get there and developing patterns and habits to support that end result.

Leadership

220. **You will lead**-In order to obtain power over your future you will have to be a leader. In the most minimal sense, you will have to lead yourself through whatever you are facing. In time you may feel inspired to share what you learn with others.

221. **Everyone is a leader**-Every person who strives for independence will become a leader. There are people who only follow the commands and advice of others so by simply taking the action to lead your own life you are being a leader.

222. **Leaders have passion**-Passion is the power that is going to drive you to make the changes you need to make and ask the right questions. Passion breeds curiosity and curiosity creates growth.

223. **Leaders love**-Love is the compassion and empathy required to want to understand those that you are leading. Love can be firm and have boundaries, but it is recommended to be an engaged leader.

224. **Lead life, don't question it**-Some people will be afraid to ever step outside of their comfort zones. They will always be controlled by what others think. Introspection is important but, if you want to lead your life you will have to move past questioning everything you want to do. This is not something everyone is willing to do. Some people will forever be dictated by the world around them.

225. **Encourage others**-Encourage others by highlighting their accomplishments. Make it a point to identify and recognize when people perform well. When you do this, you will find that people radiate towards you and want to hear what you have to say.

226. **Show others their value**-Show genuine interest and appreciation for the presence and ideas of others. When someone talks, take time to listen to what they have to say. Don't cut people off when they are talking and show more attention to what they have to say than what you want to say.

227. **Inspire others**-People inherently want to feel valued. Encourage people to think outside of the box and appreciate the ideas they come to you with. Be open minded to what others have to say so that they know you and working together and part of the same team.

228. **Leadership has no number**-Remember that if you only influence one person or 1 million people you are still having an impact on someone. That impact always carries value no matter the number of people behind it. The way you influence people will radiate to others. Even if you are only inspiring one person, you are still a leader.

Organization

229. **The power of organization**-Organization is a crucial component to creating the life that you want to live. If you're not organized its hard create a process that empowers you and enables you to track your progress. Having structure in your life will give you a series of reference points to measure your growth in different aspects of your life.

230. **Prioritize**-Developing a plan can feel overwhelming if you've never done it before. Start with whatever things are most important to your life. Think about your most immediate goal and begin identifying the steps it takes to get there. After you do this with your highest priority, you can do this with whatever comes next on the list of importance to you.

231. **You don't have to do it all**-As you go through the process of organizing your priorities by importance you are eventually going to come to one of two points. The first being when you find something matters so little that it does not seem worth the effort of organization or the second being that you no longer have time to devote energy to it. This is natural. You simply may not be able to devote the amount of energy you want to everything that you are going to want to do. Don't beat yourself up over this.

232. **Priorities change**-As time progresses you may not feel the same motivation with some of your priorities that you felt in the past. This may be because your interests or level of interests are changing. It may also happen when you have begun to master of one your target goals. When this happen, it may be time to change the amount of effort you're putting into your interests. You may even be able to remove one interest in place of another.

233. **Pace yourself**-You're not going to be able to accomplish everything you want overnight, and if you do, you're going to lose a lot of sleep over it. Keep this in mind. Everything you do will have an impact on the rest of your life. Enjoy the process of growing and keep things in perspective if you begin to feel behind or overwhelmed.

234. **The number one priority**-There are a lot of things that you can set out to accomplish. But few things will last forever, and few objective things mean as much to people as they think they will. The one thing that will always exist is how you feel and exist in the world. So, prioritize your human experience. This means prioritize your happiness, connections, and understanding of how you exist and flow in the world. If you don't do this, you could have immeasurable objective possessions and they will all mean very little if your spirit is not intact.

235. **Work with the flow**-When developing new patterns start with the smallest changes first. Start with changes that most closely conform to your current schedule. Going with the behaviors you've already set and making small changes from them decreases the amount of resistance you will experience.

236. **Celebrate small victories**-Celebrating the little victories gives you small boosts of positive reinforcement throughout your journey that work to encourage you to continue to move forward. When you wake up on time, finish reading an article, or learn something new take a moment to appreciate that.

237. **Create systems**-One action you can take that is going to set you ahead in regard to being organized is creating systems. Create and fine tune systems to help you accomplish your goals as fast and efficiently as possible. The great news is there are probably already systems created for whatever tasks you are trying to manage. You're likely just a short search away from finding a system that is going to cut hours of monotonous work into a quick and efficient process.

Goal setting

238. **Having a can do mentality**-Have you ever reflected on what you are truly capable of? More so do you find that you often doubt your ability to do something? If this is the case take a hard look at the objectives you seek and dissect what it took for other people to accomplish them. Have you found that they did anything superhuman to get where they are? If not you then you too can accomplish whatever you desire through the same ways and processes that other people have.

239. **Know your why**-Generally momentum is created because you are either being driven toward something or away from something. This

is where motivation often comes from so if you do not know your "why" reflect on what you may be driven away from or towards.

240. **How to set a goal-**Setting a goal is about reverse planning. Identify where you want to end up and what it is you want to do and plan backwards to the point that you are currently at. You should have a strong general idea of the steps you should take as well as obstacles you may encounter before you partake in an endeavor.

241. **Why to set a goal-** When you set a goal make sure it is authentic to your desires. Make sure you're not doing something for someone else or because you feel like you have too.

242. **Stay the course-**The modern world is one of constant stimulation. It can be easy to get distracted or discouraged. Just like you have made a commitment of growth to yourself you have to make a commitment toward growing toward your goals. It will not always be easy but through consistency and commitment you can come out on top.

Perception

243. **The power of perception-**Your outlook on the word is the first thing that gears you toward fulfilling or empty experiences. The following are some examples of a few specific outlooks that you may carry with you to ensure you have the most enjoyment in life. This is only a small sample of the situations where your awareness and open mindedness can drastically impact your experience.

244. **Treat everyone the same-**Be cognoscente of the perception you have when you meet someone new. If you carry preconceived ideas about people, you are robbing yourself of incredible opportunities. Meet every person with the same open and curious mind.

245. **Everyone is interesting**-Everyone is interesting. No two people have lived the same lives or carried the same interests. Everyone has a unique story. Challenge yourself to learn a little bit about another person's story when time you meet someone new.

246. **You're not alone**-Be open to expressing yourself to others. You will find that even though your problems aren't always the same as others they may be similar, and you will share similar emotions about them. You are not alone.

247. **You are a gift**-Before you expect anything of anyone else think first what you are bringing to the table. Think about the ways that you can be incredible to those who have the opportunity to meet you.

248. **It's not that serious**-Many of the situations that people face are not life or death, but it gets blown up to feel that way. Relax a little and don't worry so much about the result of everything that happens.

249. **Choose the story**-You could talk to many different people that have all experienced the same event and they will all view the experience in a different way. Why is this? Because everyone focuses on different things. People pick and choose what stands out most to them. That's why one person could love the same experience that someone else did not enjoy. Pay attention to what things you focus on. Keep in mind that there may be a new way to view your experience if you devote your attention to different parts of it.

Things happen for a reason

250. **Do things happen for a reason**-You may wonder if there is a grand plan in the world that you cannot see. Does everything happen for a reason? The answer to this question may never be known but you

can choose to make sure that everything that happens serves you in some way.

251. **How to ensure everything has a purpose**-Everything that happens shifts your momentum in one way or another. Instead of using energy to constantly fight change you can learn to use challenging events as a guide to new opportunities and lessons.

252. **Be flexible**-Not everything is going to go the way you desire or plan. This isn't always a reflection or you, your process, or progress. Sometimes things just don't go according to plan. On the same note sometimes, incredible opportunities present themselves that you never expected. Keep your eyes open for these opportunities. If you're so set in your plan or ways that you fail to take advantage of new opportunities, you will miss out on unforeseen fortunes.

253. **Enjoy the ride**-At some point you're going to find yourself at what seems to be your lowest point. The worst part in your life. From this rock bottom point it's easy to become transfixed on whatever fierce set of problems you face. But obsessing on the negative things does not change the existence of your problems. Make it a practice to still appreciate the experience you are having. Take time to reflect upon the good things that still exist and event to appreciate the bad things and the situations that they introduce you too.

Balance

254. **The importance of balance**-The effects of neglecting fulfillment in one area of life will spill over and impacted other areas in your life. If you want the best performance in every aspect of your life you need to know how to have balance.

255. **How to have balance-**The first step to having balance it's under-standing what balance is and why it's important. Balance utilizes time management and discretion to provide you with the peace that enables you to have the highest level of happiness and enjoyment.

256. **Areas of balance-** The things that will determine what provides someone peace and enjoyment vary from person to person. Identify factors in your life that cause you stress and have a plan that enables you to mitigate those stressors. Reflect on your goals and have a plan that you allow you to give adequate attention to those ambi-tions, lastly and most importantly identify what things you derive enjoyment from and allow yourself to embrace them.

257. **Signs you lack balance-**When you find yourself working so hard at one area of your goals to where you devote minimal or no time to your other priorities you are lacking balance. If you feel yourself exhausted as you start something you need to reflect on if you are living a well-proportioned life.

258. **Down time-**If free time drives you crazy you may be facing a cou-ple of things. The first being that your anxiety makes you uncom-fortable with downtime. The second being that you are unable to manage everything going on in your life so downtime makes you feel guilty.

259. **The power of blank space-**Blank space, is essentially free time, and it is the template for organization that you can use to create in time for all of your goals and interests. When used right it is the pathway to accomplishing everything you desire.

260. **The picture of a balanced life-**A balanced life is one where your stress is at a minimum, you're in line with your goals, and have a

plan to achieve them. Then you give yourself the space to enjoy the journey of life and explore your interests.

Living your worst-case scenario

261. **Identifying your worst case scenario**-What is your worst case scenario? Have you identified it? Is it something that you live in constant fear of or something that you have never thought of yet? You can have multiple worst-case scenarios relating to different aspects of life. One of your scenarios may be more immediate like having serious car troubles while another may be more personal and distant like worries of not ever being loved.

262. **Living your worst-case scenario**-Is fear and anxiety constantly lingering in the back of your mind? Give yourself space to confront the thoughts you are having by thinking in detail what it would look like to go through your worst-case scenario. It could be something small like being late to work or something huge like a death in the family.

263. **Accepting your worst-case scenario**-Accept your worst-case scenario as a possibility and ask yourself is it really as bad as you're building it up to be? If it is that bad, then what steps can you take to prepare for it? If it's not what parts of it may be grossly exaggerated or unfounded?

264. **Growing from your worst-case scenario**-There are lessons to be taken from identifying your worst-case scenario. When you fully understand it, then the worst scenario can be used as a part of the planning process and a contingency rather than a panic point.

Complacency

265. **The end of growth**-Complacency is a dangerous because it is a point where you become stagnant in your growth. When you stop

challenging yourself to grow you can find yourself in a position where life passes you by because you stopped asking the questions that cause you to do things that propel you towards your next adventure.

266. **Causes of complacency**-Complacency can come from the idea that you already know everything that you need to know in a subject. Or the misconception that you already have experienced everything that you may want to experience.

267. **Conscious complacency**-Conscious complacency is when you have created a reason for why you live in a bubble. Then you continue to make excuses for why you can't leave it. Conscious complacency is so dangerous because it is something that is reinforced throughout time by making similar comfortable decisions that are backed by misguided logic. This is why it can be so hard to break out of.

268. **Unconscious complacency**-Unconscious complacency is when you are unaware of your complacency. Often, it's because you've never been introduced to the idea of what complacency is. You may have made it a habit to accept what life gives you and you may be around people who encourage that behavior. Many people live this way because they don't even realize that they have the option or ability to improve their lives.

269. **The danger of complacency**-The mental and emotional body can die long before the physical body. When you become complacent you often loose the fire that drives you and you begin to accept whatever life gives you rather than stepping into the driver's seat of your life.

270. **The power of curiosity**-Curiosity is the repellent for complacency. Stay interested in the world around you and learn from others.

Curiosity is the fuel that will propel your growth and keep you away from a complacent life.

Resistance

271. **What is resistance**-Resistance is a deep and internal feeling of opposition. Often when you experience this you it is an indicator that you are in a critical moment in your life. Something you should move toward or away from.

272. **Signs of resistance**-When you are doing the wrong things you will feel resistance residually, it will be a gnawing and consistent sort of dread. When you are doing the right things, you will also feel resistance in a different way. It will be more of an apprehension when associated with challenging yourself and facing uncharted territory.

273. **Resistance is a guide**-Resistance serves as a guide. By knowing the why of when you are feeling yourself resist things you will learn more about if what you are doing is where you should be or not. At your core you should essentially pay attention to what you are feeling and why.

274. **Follow your resistance**-Don't run just because you feel resistance. Listen to it. It has so much to tell you about where you should and shouldn't be. Your discomfort are clues to what you should challenge yourself with and what you should avoid. It's all about why you feel the discomfort.

Ego

275. **Ego**-Ego is the perception you have of yourself. It is what and who you identify as. It is important to take regular checks on what your ego is and how you are allowing it to present itself.

276. **Fear and defense**-if you find yourself existing to serve your ego you will begin to act from a place of fear. You will always be afraid that something could dissociate you from the relationship you have built with your ego and because of it you will be constantly defensive. This defensiveness leads to being close minded and furthermore stagnancy and complacency.

277. **The burden of ego**-When improperly managed ego is a huge burden. It can weigh you down as it is something you constantly seek to fulfill. It will strip you of your peace, awareness, and power as you become fixated on that chore.

278. **Avoid a reputation driven life**-Some people are trapped by a brutal cycle of constantly hoping to achieve a desired outcome for every action they take. They want to be first in a way that is crippling. It is not enough for this kind of person to exist; they expect to be number one person on other people's minds too. This is an ego driven approach to life that has no definitive fulfillment.

279. **Overcoming ego**-They key to overcoming ego is to create an ego based on principles, and morals. These are often intangible, but it gives you something to measure yourself up too. Measure yourself up to the values that you set for yourself. Not on a black and white set of accomplishments and how you compare to others.

280. **Confidence**-Confidence is when you are aware internally of what you know but do not feel the drive to constantly make an external point of what you know or trump others. This is the egos healthiest form.

Being present

281. **Experiencing the moment**-It's hard to experience the moment when your mind is crowded with thoughts the past and future. Clearing your mind of those thoughts is the first step to existing in the present.

282. **Peace with the past**-When you exist at peace with your past then you can exist at peace with your present. You should acknowledge your past as a part of you but not as the defining point of who you are or a determinant of the future.

283. **Peace with the future**-You can exist at peace with your future when you have a process that gives you the ability to influence your future. Along with this baseline process you should identify and develop skill sets that you think will give you power to impact the future. As you create these processes you should be willing to give yourself the peace to live in the moment, knowing that you are doing the most that you can for yourself.

284. **Thoughts that take away from being present**-Unresolved emotions inhibit you from being present. One aspect of your life will influence the other, if you want to be able to be present you will have to manage other aspects of your life.

285. **Desire inhibits pleasure**-If you are always measuring up experiences for what you accomplish or take from them then you will limit yourself from being able to enjoy that moment for whatever it is. Be careful not to find yourself seeking forms of pleasure in everything you do. If you do this in time the pleasure will decrease but your desire for it will not.

Introspection

286. **The why of introspection**-Introspection is the practice of being self-aware. It's how you become aware of your own thoughts as well as the world around you.

287. **The use of introspection**-Use introspection as a way to understand, solve problems, and identify your future goals. Introspection has so much value and many different purposes. The most important is that it brings you in touch with yourself. It gives you the ability to be aware.

288. **Pay attention to your mood**-Be aware of your mood. What are your thoughts when you start your day and as you go through your day? Are you optimistic or do you find yourself with negative beliefs about how your day will go? What can you do to orient your belief system to one that will best serve you as you go throughout your day?

289. **Your perception of others**-What is your belief system when it comes to people? Do you see others as a burden who may be "out to get you" and hold you back or do you see people as an extension of your experience and opportunity in life? Where does your beliefs about others come from and do you want it to look like? What practice do you need to have to change your beliefs about people?

290. **Your perception of yourself**-How do you view yourself? Do you believe you are valuable and capable, or do you feel helpless and unworthy? Are you in control of your thoughts about yourself or do you need to take some time to focus on the perception you have of yourself?

291. **Your perception of opportunity**-Do you think that opportunity exists? Do you think you have the ability to find it? Or do you instead think that fortune is scarce and not meant for you? What can you do to draw in the opportunities that you desire?

292. **Practice positivity**-Turn your gratitude into a practice. Intentionally focus on the thing's that you can find to be grateful for. Find things from large to small that are enjoyable, or exciting and worth waking up for. It may seem odd at first, but this practice will become addicting after a while, and it will change your outlook on the world. Be warry of the other end of this practice which involves focusing on the negative aspects of your life.

293. **Your outlook on life**-How are you viewing the world and your experience? Are you hopeful? Or are you afraid? What experiences can you create to give yourself the best outlook on the world?

The decision making process

294. **Measure your decisions**-A lot of the trouble that people find themselves in is because they don't have a process when it comes to making decisions. They think mainly of the immediate desire or feelings they are having and not at all about the consequences. Here are some thoughts to measure your actions up to before you take them.

295. **The immediate result**-What is the immediate result of the action you are about to take? What is your intended result? Is it to make a point? Could it be to accomplish a goal? Or is it instead a means to an end? Ask yourself what you want to accomplish with your immediate action and if or how it will accomplish that goal.

296. **The future of the action**-What is the long-term effect of your action, and actions? Are the things you're doing solving a more

immediate desire but maybe drawing you away from your long-term objectives? Are your actions directed at helping you accomplish your long-term goals at all?

297. **The absence of the result**-Now consider what would happen if you didn't make a certain decision? Would not taking an action have terrible consequences? Or perhaps does not taking a certain action benefit you more than taking it?

Life compounders

298. **Life compounders**-There are certain decisions you can make in your life that will carry heavy consequences that will last for a long while. Understanding, preventing, and managing these things can greatly impact your quality of life.

299. **Debt**-if you put yourself in debt that does not work for you then you may find yourself a slave to that debt. It can put you in situations where you are forced to put your needs second to your obligation.

300. **Records**-Keeping a good record is important. Anything that carries a record impacts your ability to access certain things in the future. By maintaining a good record, you avoid the limits created by a bad record.

301. **Contracts**-Be cautious with the things that you can commit to. If you make the wrong commitment, you can find yourself in situations that are hard to break out of no matter how much they drain from you. A binding contract is the worst kind of commitment to be held to if it ends up being a burden.

Energy

302. **Energy Management**-Few things are more frustrating than expending your energy in ways that render no result. Taking action alone does not guarantee a desired result. On the same note focusing large amounts of time on something never guarantees completion or mastery. You have to make regular checkups to ensure that the time and energy you spend towards the things that you want to create is being spent in the most efficient ways. The following chapter lists common things to be cognoscente of as you go through your day.

303. **Work does not guarantee productivity**-Just because you are physically doing work does not mean you are actually being productive. If you want to measure how productive your work is then pay attention to the amount of time you are wasting on the job when you are distracted and get sidetracked. It is more fair to yourself to only spend the minimal time you need to be productive on your tasks and devote the rest of the time that you spend distracted to other things that interest you.

304. **Is your recreation relaxing**-Make sure that the time that you set aside to enjoy yourself is rejuvenating. To measure how relaxing your time off is pay attention to how much your mind wonders into stressful thoughts when you should be present and relaxed. If your mind is always on negative things when you should be feeling rejuvenated, you need to take time to address this and find out if you need to find a better outlet or if you need to manage your unresolved emotions.

305. **Talking is not always communication**-When you are communicating it is important that you and the person you are in communication with are being heard. If you want to measure how effective your communication is ensure that the point that you are trying

to communicate is being listened to and understood. Likewise do the same for those that you are in communication with. It is possible to talk about something for eternity yet never reach a result. Communication is a practice and unless both people are open to and engaged in that practice energy will be wasted.

306. **Prioritize your interests**-In anything you do make sure you are prioritizing yourself and your interests. Make sure you are leveraging your efforts in ways that help you get as close as you want to where you want to be and what you want to do.

307. **Everything has a price**-Everything you do costs you something. Keep this in mind before you commit to anything. Most things at the least can be fundamentally measured in time or energy. This is a limited resource.

308. **What is your price**-Do you know what your price is? You should have a point where you are able acknowledge that whatever you are pursuing is no longer with the time and energy being spent anymore. Only use your resources where they are best spent.

309. **Your energy should return itself**-Your energy is best spent in ways that return itself. When you are spending your time and energy on the right things you will feel rejuvenated. You will feel your energy being multiplied rather than drained. What kind of things multiply your energy and what kind of unnecessarily things drain it?

310. **The practice of utilization**-Using your energy in ways that support and serve you is a practice. You must be aware of how your actions affect your energy and have a plan on how you could best use your energy to serve yourself and your future. This will never be a perfect process as it is a continuous practice.

Time

311. **The perception of time**-The perception people have of time determines their outlook on many other things. It directly impacts stress and happiness in many situations. Creating a relationship with time that serves you will help you live you best quality of life.

312. **Time as a comparison**-Very often the relationship that people have to time is one where they compare where someone else is at in a certain amount of time versus where they are at. This is the worst relationship to have with time because it takes no other factors into consideration. It's a one-sided comparison that creates countless negative emotions.

313. **Time as a measuring tool**-Time as the comparison does not exist. Time alone as a measuring tool is inaccurate. It's single faceted and does not factor the intangible growth, education and other progress that occurs while going through the journey of life.

314. **Measuring yourself against yourself**-The most accurate indicator of your progress is using time to compare yourself against yourself. But this is not only a hard measurement. You should also measure the intangibles in your life to see how they've changed. Are you feeling better? Are you happier? Do you have deeper connections? When you compare yourself against yourself make sure that you are taking the full picture into consideration.

Community

315. **Community is key**-Having a community is an important part of life. It can impact your happiness, productivity, and growth. If you are around the right community those things will flourish. If you are around the wrong community, it can feel impossible to have those

things. Take note of the community that you choose. This section covers a few tips on how to find your community and ensure it is the right one for you.

316. **Community is a mentality**-Community has to do with how you relate to the world around you and where you fit in. This can be a set of beliefs that exists in your mind. You can approach the world with a sense of community. The principles of a good community can be found anywhere. Rather than hoping to find community you can bring the concept of community to wherever you go. Envision what community is too you and look for it wherever you are. The standards of an ideal community will be different to everyone. This section poses some ideas and questions on what that community is to you.

317. **Community is a feeling**-You should feel a sense of community when you are in the right environments. How do you want to feel from your community and how does your current community make you feel? How do you find or create a community that is in line with your vision?

318. **Community is everywhere**-Your community does not have to be a certain group of people at a certain time every week. You can find community in a one time conversation or in phone conversations with friends. Community can be found in so many unconventional ways.

319. **Community should rejuvenate you**-The community you chose should rejuvenate you. After spending time in it you should feel refreshed and ready to attack your goals.

320. **Community should listen to you**-When you are in the right community you will find people who listen openly to you without

judgment. You will ideally find that these people can present you with new ideas to help you tackle problems you are facing and expand your thinking.

321. **Community should support you**-Most of all your community should support you. Your community should not belittle you, or make you feel like you are a burden.

Pillars of Success-

322. **Replication of quality results**-Having success in one area of your life is not an accident. It is the collection of good decision and habits that propel you to be successful. Because success is a matter of principles and standards you can use the skills that you would use to be successful in one area of your life to be successful in other areas. This chapter outlines some of the skills that it takes to find that success.

323. **Patience**-The most vital characteristic you must have is understanding and patience. You must be patient with yourself, your process, and the progress you make. Not everything will happen in the time you desire, and you will fall short of the standards you have set at times, but patience is the commitment to yourself to hold through those moments of friction that you encounter for the benefit of completing the bigger picture.

324. **Time management**-Properly managing your time makes it possible to prioritize your goals in a structured way that gives you time to partake in them. More so proper time management set you up to be in a position where you can be productive with your time when you are using it to better yourself.

325. **Organization**-You must be organized. Proper organization is the framework to accomplishing tasks. Being organized enables you to understand the steps needed to accomplish your goals from start to finish. Organization is the process of setting prioritizing the order that steps come in in order to take process from start to finish.

326. **Discipline**-Discipline is the backbone to your success. Discipline is the fortitude to go through with the plans you set when and how you set them.

327. **Passion**-Passion is the fire that keeps you curious and hungry to continue learning. Passion should come naturally when you're doing what you are meant to be doing. But it may wane with time. If this happens take a step back to reflect on why you are doing what you are doing.

328. **Clear communication**-In anything you do you need to have clear and proper communication with those you work with. The right people are a vital part of any process. Knowing how to communicate with them can circumvent and help you overcome many obstacles.

329. **Consistency**-The key to replicating success is consistency. Consistency both in your practice of using good habits, as well as your commitment to understanding whatever endeavor you choose to partake in. You will never be able see the results of your actions if you do not allow yourself to show up day after day to improve and grow.

Working past problems

330. **Contact plan**-You're going to run into challenging situations in life. Accepting that is the first step to overcoming these events. Sometimes the challenge you are facing may feel like a wall that you

can't find a way through or around. This chapter goes over a few of the approaches that you can take in order to make it past these walls.

331. **Take a step back**-When you're feeling overwhelmed by a problem take a moment to distance yourself from it. Maybe you need time, or space, maybe both. But take what the appropriate measures to give yourself what's necessary so you can view the problem objectively.

332. **Identify the problem**-Make sure you fully understand the problem you are encountering. Try to cut away the parts that don't matter, or matter least if possible. This way you know that you are devoting your time and energy to the appropriate task.

333. **Assess your approach**-Examine the actions you're taking to solve the problem. Is it the best course possible? Perhaps is your approach part of the problem?

334. **Consider new solutions**-Are there different approaches that you could take that would help manage the problem? Could you avoid the problem all together? Could a new person or resource bring a new idea to solve the problem?

Take control of your surroundings

335. **What do you surround yourself with**-Take a moment to reflect on your surroundings. Is your environment by choice or accident? Are you consciously choosing what you surround yourself with or have you absently ended up where you are? In order to mold the future, you want you need to take note of your surroundings and how they compare with your ideal environment that would best support you.

336. **Choosing your environment**-Do you have the option to choose your environment? Can you choose to be in areas without the negative influences you are avoiding? Can you choose to be away from

the people who may hold you back? Reflect on if these are options that you should take in order to gain control of your surroundings.

337. **Creating your environment**-If you can not find an environment that fulfills and supports you then take the initiative to create one in your image. Invite people that you want to be around to places that you want to be at.

Food for thought

338. **Don't become fixed on the negative things**-Pay attention to the amount proportion of time you spend having negative thoughts compared to positive thoughts. If you find yourself spending more time in a negative mindset, make it a priority to stop and find out why and how you can change that.

339. **Decision management**-If you're uncertain of a decision you should make don't feel awkward literally talking yourself through the options. Weighing out the negatives and positives of each until you feel like you are able to walk yourself on whichever one best serves you.

340. **Mastering key moments**-The morning is a vital point in the day because how you start your day forms your outlook on how you view the rest of your day and your ability to handle it. Starting key moments right will leave you feeling accomplished and grounded. This gives you a pivot point for the rest of the day. What the "right morning" looks like is different from person to person. One person may want to start the morning in a hyper productive way in contrast someone else may feel accomplished by beginning the morning in a relaxed manner. Key moments are not limited to your morning though. Set aside certain times in the day, week, or month and make

it a point to use them in a way that is fulfilling to you. This will keep you grounded and feeling successful.

341. **Stop and appreciate the moment**-Stop and enjoy the moment you're in. Understand that it has a purpose. Allow yourself to be relieved of thoughts of the future and past and connect deeper with the experience you are having in the present.

342. **Live every day as if it was your first**-Be curious about the world around you. Be open minded to the idea that you have not experienced everything there is to experience. Try taking on each experience as if it were the first time. Allow yourself to experience it with the curiosity, pleasure, and open mind that you did the first time you had the experience.

343. **Focus on what is**-A frequent cause of dissatisfaction is being focused on what a moment could be rather than appreciating what it is. When this happens you may find yourself upset because you cannot change things that you want to change. Understand the futility of these thoughts and start to instead think about what the current experience you're having is providing you.

344. **Life is the practice**-People often think that they are supposed to set aside time to practice productive habits. But when they come back to their day to day life and the practice period ends, they use little to none of what they were learning. The reality is day to day life is the practice of the things that you want to create and the ways you want to behave. So, decide what you want to change and start doing it now. It may not always go perfectly, and it won't happen overnight, but the best way to make something happen is by turning it into a regular practice in your day to day life.

345. **The practice of mistakes**-No matter what happens and how far you move forward you will still find yourself making mistakes occasionally. It is a natural part of growth no matter how long you have been doing something. It serves as a way to continue to mold you where you are soft and reinforce the productive ideas that you practice.

346. **Accepting your humanity**-Accept the fact that you are human, and you are having a human experience. Being human means having moments that are imperfect and awkward. It means that you aren't going to line up perfectly with every person you meet and that you will not always crush every challenge you face.

Be a Creator

347. **You have power**-You should now be aware that you are not meant to be limited by the vicissitudes of the world. No longer should you be thrown around by the currents of friction. You have the power to create anything you desire. Everyone on some level is made to be a creator. Your ideas are unique, and your presence is a gift to others. As a gift to yourself and the world you should go forth and create what you are meant to build.

348. **Where is your mind**-Check in with your habits, and thoughts. No longer should you be driven by unconscious behaviors. Think about where you are spending your energy and what you use your time to think about. Focus your mind on the ideas and affirmations that are going to enable you to mold the product that you are here to make.

349. **Be intentional**-Use your resources consciously. Think before you act and allow your actions to flow together in ways that produce for you.

350. **Think**-Think without limits. Think without the constraint of size or time. Your creations should not be limited by either of those factors. What you create is not a question of if, but of how.

Service to Others

351. **Service**-Many questions exist about the existence of the world and how humans came to earth, and why they exist. There are many different ideas on the answers to these questions. Despite all the possible answers the fact is that humans are real and exist. All around you are people existing in their experience in the best way that they know how. Because of this, there is no greater act than that of providing something positive to someone else's experience. Because for them, the value that you added in that moment is real, and it may have been just what they needed to inspire them on to the next step of their journey.

352. **The Purpose of Creation**-This is why being a creator is so important. When you explore your passions and gifts, it doesn't just add to you it adds onto the entire world. When you share your gift, you possibly inspire someone else to consider something they did not know, or to explore their own talents.

353. **A Connected World**-Though everyone's experience is different the world as a whole is connected. The actions of one may inspire another to think, or act differently, and in turn those actions will spread among others. The effects of setting a good example are limitless.

354. **The highlight reel**-What if your actions don't affect the entire world? That doesn't make it worthless. When you involve someone in the sharing of your passions it may not change the entire world, but it may have been the best experience of their world at that

moment. It may have no impact at all, but it may have a profound impact that they will never forget.

355. **Profound influences-**The collection of stimulating experiences from person after person is bound to wake someone up to the possibility of a different kind of life. A life where they can be driven by passion, instead of trapped in the motions of monotony.

356. **Acts of service-**Your actions do not have to be divine. Your actions do not even always need to be a reflection of your gift. Your actions only need to be pure to open the eyes of others. You will influence people not only by what you do but also how you do it. Live your life in a way that inspires others even when you are not making a definitive move. Every act of service performed with sincerity opens the eyes of someone to a new way of living.

357. **Sincerely You-**There is so much friction in the day to day life of many people that they are reduced to a state of simply existing. Of going through the motions without vigor. Acting from a place of genuine emotion and concern is one of the best things that you can do. This example can implore others to consider that they too can live with a life separate from their friction.

Your Practice

358. **You must have a practice-**None of the ideas in this book will carry any value to you if you do not practice them. The idea of personal growth is not something that can be thought about once and mastered. It is a changing, growing, and fluid thing. Turn anything you want to be proficient at into a practice, especially your thoughts and behaviors.

359. **Make your practice personal**-It's possible that none of the ideas in this book apply to you. But if you read this book, you likely care about personal growth and are on a journey related to that. Find whatever concepts, behaviors and thoughts suite you and use those for your practice. Everyone's practice will be different.

360. **Practice makes more practice**-Perfection does not exist. Any skill that one becomes proficient in is the result of a commitment to practice and reflection. So don't take beat yourself up when you find that you still make mistakes sometimes, after years of doing something.

361. **Reflect**-Take regular intervals to reflect on how the ideas you are practicing serve you. Make sure they are still relevant to the person that you are in the present.

362. **Grow your practice**-As you grow your practice should grow. Some parts of your practice may stay consistent throughout your life. Other's may need to change based on what your priorities are at the moment.

The Journey's Close

363. **Stay the course**-There were a lot of ideas in this book. Maybe they were new to you, maybe not. As stated at the start of this book, the process of personal growth and improving your mental health is a journey. Not a destination that ends with this book. Use the ideas in this book to make your journey more smooth but always be on the lookout for new concepts that will drive your growth.

364. **Remember your resources**-This book does not have all the answers. Though it ideally provides many solutions, and skill sets to find the answers you need it does not have all of them. Keep your mind open

for whatever resources you think you may need on your journey and most importantly never be afraid to reach out for help when you're at a tough spot.

365. **Thank you**-Lastly, thank you. Thank you for reading this book, but more so thank you for listening to yourself. Thank you for being open to the idea that you needed to make your mental health a priority and thank you for having the strength to do that.

Closing Remarks

Like anyone sometimes I wonder what the purpose of life may be, and how much control people have over that purpose. I have observed and gathered a few consistencies based on my life and the lives of others. What I have learned is that life is a journey, and that journey is the purpose of life. In that journey humans are made to explore their hobbies and interests. People are made to connect with and serve others all in their own way. I have also seen that people have lived "multiple lives" meaning that the ideas and behaviors that define a person at one age or period of their life may be completely different in the next phase of their live. For this reason, it is not possible to live life as a destination because you are always learning and growing. For this reason, I encourage you as the reader to enjoy your journey and never consider that you have reached the end of road.

About the author

I grew up in a small town. At times I was uncertain if I would have the opportunity to leave it. So, joined the Marine Corps Infantry after high school, and for the first time I saw mountains. I wasn't even sure they had existed, or that I would ever be afforded the luxury to see them. Because of my service I was encouraged to think bigger. I've traveled to over 10 different countries on my personal time. Then I began to feel called to serve as a paramedic. Working in life and death has given me a unique perspective on life. I carry the most empathy for those who are living but are unable to access what they want in life. I have been so blessed to experience and continue to experience things that I have never dreamed of. I want that same future for others, and that is why I have written this book.

CONTACT INFORMATION

Please contact me in any of the following ways:

Email: mentalhealth365ways@outlook.com
Website: mentalhealth365ways.com
Twitter: Mentalhealth365ways
Instagram: mentalhealth365ways
Facebook group: Mentalhealth365ways

#mentalhealth365ways

I may not know you, and I may never have the opportunity to meet you, but I know that your story is so important. I know that I have something to learn from you and so does the rest of the world. I encourage you to share a part of your story by posting a meaningful picture of yourself and #mental-health365ways and tag the Instagram page. What I want from you is to share a part of your story. It can be a tip that you think others could use to find happiness, or a story from your life, or even one of your passions. Regardless it is important, and someone needs to hear it. We all have much to learn from each other and that starts with global transparency.